INTO A RAGING SEA

INTO A RAGING SEA

MY LIFE AND THE *PENDLETON* RESCUE

By Bernard C. Webber
Introduction by Michael J. Tougias

On
Cape Publications
Cape Cod, MA

*The line drawings in this book are by Paul C. Morris
of Nantucket, Massachusetts.*

This book is dedicated to my wife,
MIRIAM,
"Who Waited"

The Rescue: This is an artist's conception of the scene offshore on 18 February 1952 at about 7:30 p.m., five miles off Chatham, when the motor lifeboat CG36500 went to the rescue of thirty-two men aboard the broken stern half of the tanker Pendleton.

—Painting by George A. Robbins, Harwich, Massachusetts.

Contents

ACKNOWLEDGMENTS

I AM DEEPLY GRATEFUL to the many individuals who encouraged me to write this book and to those who offered their talents and skills to assist in making it become a reality. I am indebted to many people.

In particular I'm grateful to Bill Quinn who besides supplying pictures, took charge of production and publication of the first edition of this book in 1985 and brought everything to completion. A special thanks goes to John Ullman who took on the monumental task of editing the manuscript for the first edition of this book in 1985. I am most appreciative of Dick Kelsey and Ed Semprini and their efforts in helping me to tell much of the story by their written recollections of events and through the use of some of the famous Kelsey photos. It is with a deep sense of appreciation and pride I acknowledge the work in the book by Paul C. Morris, noted Nantucket marine artist, author and ivory carver.

Again, to all those who took time out from their already busy lives to generously help me, my heartfelt thanks.

FOREWORD

BERNIE WEBBER ORIGINALLY PUBLISHED THIS BOOK with Lower Cape Publishing Company in 1985 under the title *Chatham, The Lifeboatmen.* The book was part autobiography and part history, with a good deal of focus on the incredible rescue of the men onboard the oil tanker *Pendleton.* Bernie and his crew performed that rescue at night in a raging sea. The book had a modest print run and did not remain in print long. Interest in Bernie Webber and his rescue, however, was reignited in 2009 when my co-written book, *The Finest Hours: The True Story of the Coast Guard's Most Daring Sea Rescue,* was released, and still more attention arose when the Disney Corporation made a movie based on *The Finest Hours.*

Bernie's daughter, Pattie Hamilton, had received many inquiries about the possibility of her father's book being reprinted, and Pattie discussed the matter with me. I conferred with publisher Adam Gamble, and the two of us carefully reread *The Lifeboatmen.* We realized the book was a real gem but thought it was mistitled. Here was the story of Bernie's life, with the emphasis on his many years and varied duties in the Coast Guard. It is the story of sacrifice, bravery, disappointments, challenges, and accomplishments. In the background of Bernie's journey was one constant—the sea.

At the age of sixteen, after Bernie dropped out of school, he enlisted in the US Maritime Service. This began years of working on or near the sea— years that included adventure, close calls, and hair-raising rescues, many of which occurred when the seas turned into rampaging, avalanching mountains. We decided to retitle the book to reflect what was at its core: Bernie's willingness to enter raging seas to rescue those in peril.

Most people familiar with the name Bernie Webber associate him with the miraculous rescue of thirty-two men off of the stern of the *Pendleton* after the ship had split in two, not far from the shores of Cape Cod during a winter storm in 1952. Rescuing thirty-two sailors from a sinking ship is a dramatic tale, but what made this mission so special is that the boat Bernie skippered that terrible night was a mere thirty-six feet in length and the waves were almost twice that size! Bernie and his crew, composed of Andy Fitzgerald, Irving Maske, and Richard Livesey, performed one of the most remarkable feats in maritime history. How those four crewmen made it over the thundering Chatham Bar, located the tanker without so much as a compass, then saved the lives of thirty-two out of the thirty-three men trapped on the foundering *Pendleton* is the stuff of legend. And how they managed to make it back to safe harbor in that tiny thirty-six-foot rescue boat (riding low in the breaking seas, loaded with a total of thirty-six men) is just as remarkable.

In *Into a Raging Sea*, Bernie tells that story, but the book is so much more than that; just as Bernie's life was so much more than one famous rescue. In these pages, you'll read about rescue attempts that did not turn out well, stories of fishermen from a Cape Cod long past, rescues done with the bygone technique of breeches buoy, humorous anecdotes, and what Cape Cod and its people meant to Bernie.

• • •

BERNIE'S LIFE AND MY OWN INTERSECTED in 2004 through our mutual interest in maritime history. I had begun writing books about true survival-at-sea ordeals when I stumbled upon a Coast Guard Marine Board of Investigation chronicling how angry seas ripped in half both the *Pendleton* and *Fort Mercer*, and the multiple rescue attempts that ensued. The story fascinated me, and I began to read through every newspaper article and document associated with the incident that I could find. Then I moved on to locating people involved in the rescue, and of course that led me to Bernie. This was a couple years before I teamed up with coauthor Casey Sherman to write the book.

I called Bernie, introduced myself, and told him I was working on a manuscript about the *Pendleton* and *Fort Mercer* rescues, thinking he'd jump at the chance to be involved. Instead, he surprised me by saying he wasn't interested, explaining that he'd done enough interviews with journalists and that he didn't think there would be a market for the book I was proposing.

I was crushed. I had just spent the last year learning everything I could about the event, but without Bernie's involvement in the project, the manuscript would never be complete. Instead of saying goodbye, I started to tell Bernie what I had learned about the *Fort Mercer* rescue. We talked for almost an hour, with me mixing in questions to Bernie about his *Pendleton* rescue. When the conversation came to an end, Bernie still wasn't wild about being involved in the project, but he was gracious and kept the door open…a crack.

A couple years later when I made the wise decision to team up with Casey Sherman to write the story, I called Bernie again, and, like before, he thought the two of us were spinning our wheels. We didn't know it at the time, but the rescue had left some emotional scars on Bernie. Who could blame him for not wanting to relive it? But as before, he took time out of his own research and writing for a book about lightships to answer my questions. After we hung up, I sent him a copy of my book *Ten Hours Until Dawn*.

I called him a month later with more questions and asked if he had enjoyed *Ten Hours*.

"Yes, it was a good read," he said.

"Great! Will you work with Casey and me on the *Pendleton* and *Fort Mercer* project?"

"Probably not."

Crushed again. I was throwing pitches, and he wasn't swinging. But we still had a nice talk, and this time I picked up flashes of his humor. So when we finished our call, I sent him another book of mine that had nothing to do with the sea but included plenty of humor, *There's A Porcupine in My Outhouse.*

I called him a month later. "Did you read *Porcupine*?"

"Yup, made me laugh, thank you."

"Great. Will you work with us on your story?"

This time there was a long pause. To the best of my memory, Bernie responded by saying something like, "Well, at least you're not full of B.S. And you're damn persistent. And you've already invested a bunch of time doing research."

"Is that a 'yes'?" I asked.

"Well," he said, "let's do it on a trial basis and see how things go."

I wished I had asked Bernie if he was testing me, to see if I was really committed to the endeavor. But whatever the reason for his change of heart, it sure was a relief for Casey and me to have Bernie on board. The time Bernie devoted to our project was lengthy, and he showed real patience with our many questions and ideas. The one point he was emphatic about was that we examine the actions of—and give credit to—other coastguardmen who played a role in the *Pendleton* rescue. An example was skipper Donald Bangs and crew, who tried to rescue men marooned on the bow of the ship. Bernie also made it clear that his own crew of Andy, Ervin, and Richard played just as an important role as he did on that fateful night. After the rescue the Coast Guard brass wanted to give Bernie the Gold Life Saving Medal and award his crew the Silver Lifesaving Medal. Bernie responded that his crew was just as deserving of the top medal, and he said, "If they can't get the gold, then I don't want it!" His crew got the gold.

After our manuscript was complete and it was at the publisher for editing and design, I was having a phone conversation with Bernie and told him my dream was to see this story turned into a movie. "Well," he said, "you keep on dreaming. But if there is a movie, Don Knotts can play my part."

Besides giving equal credit to many others involved in the rescue, Bernie lavished praise on his rescue boat, numbered 36500. That little boat was what allowed Bernie and crew to perform their remarkable rescue, and he never forgot it. In an email to Casey and I dated January 22, 2009, Bernie sent us photos of the 36500 and wrote, "Guys—here's your boat—if a movie is made, she'll be ready, just like brand new. I won't be around but give her a kiss for me."

Two days later, Bernie passed away at his home.

Well, Bernie, I went down to the Cape and gave the 36500 a kiss like you asked. A couple of tourists wondered what I was doing, but I know what that boat and the people who restored it meant to you. It's an honor to help bring your book back in print. And, oh, did I tell you Disney made a movie about your rescue? Chris Pine plays you. I think that is a better fit than Don Knotts.

—Michael J. Tougias,
Coauthor of *The Finest Hours*
www.michaeltougias.com

PROLOGUE

MY WIFE, MIRIAM, AND I had driven three days to visit and honor an old friend. Discarded, no longer considered fit for work, she somehow survived the burning fate of sisters gone before. Many years she had lain amid the swirling sands and scrub at a desolate place in Wellfleet on Cape Cod, Massachusetts, holding herself together while awaiting she knew not what.

Representing true public service of another period, somewhat stout with strength beyond compare, she had survived the ravages of time. Found where she lay, recognized as to who she was and aware of her many accomplishments during her active life, a dedicated group had resurrected her and given her fresh beauty and new purpose.

Who was this lady, this queen? What was the occasion for which a large crowd gathered beside Cape Cod waters to view and celebrate her rebirth? Awaiting her arrival, one sensed excitement in the cool Cape Cod air. The sun peeked out between the clouds, as if to view the scene.

There she was, rounding the corner into view. My heart pounded, and my eyes filled with tears. I had not seen her for nearly twenty years. And now there she was, every bit as I remembered her. Perhaps even more beautiful. A cheer went up from the crowd as she stopped in full view for all to see. The admiration for her build and her beauty was obvious on their smiling faces.

Town officials then spoke words of praise for her service and about those she served so valiantly in the pursuit of saving human lives. This day was not to be theirs alone. For among the gathering were those who brought her new life, new direction, new meaning. For them, there was a feeling of pride and accomplishment in the work they had done. The results of their efforts were now before them, for all to see and admire.

Monday, 22 June 1982 will be remembered as the day for the rebirth of this no ordinary lady. A lady in all respects, but not of the human species. She was, and continues to be, known only as CG36500, just a plain old Coast Guard motorized lifeboat to most. To some, she represents much more, and they recall the time when these little vessels were the prime means of saving lives at sea and remember the men who served in them. The perilous times and conditions in which, together, they plied dark, cold stormy waters in the quest for saving people in need. To them, she is more than just a number.

On this day, the task accepted by Town of Orleans Historical Society—to procure and restore the little boat—was complete. Many prominent and ordinary people's support for the project resulted in the successful completion of the undertaking—an epic story that should be told by them. The fruits of their labor paid off. Recommissioned and allowed to retain, by law, the only name known to her, CG36500 was launched into the waters at Rock Harbor, Orleans, Massachusetts. She continues to float in her normal environment and her natural waters, a tribute to human achievement, past and present.*

Inspired by their efforts and asked by many to relate my close association with this little boat, it becomes necessary to go back to the beginning. It was 1946 when I first saw her. Further, I need to tell you about the place, the people, and the arena in which she and others like her served so well for so many years.

To do so, I will start with the beginning, at a place where I served the public for many years on three separate occasions—simply called Chatham, that elbow of Cape Cod land bordered by the sea.

At the time of the republication of this book, 2016, the CG36500 can still be visited and viewed summers in Rock Harbor in Orleans.

Aerial view of the Chatham Coast Guard station as seen in the mid-1950s after it was remodeled. Note the lookout tower in front of the lighthouse. The number "42" is an aerial identification sign.

1

Introduction to the Community

The town of Chatham, Massachusetts, located on Cape Cod, has always been influenced by the sea surrounding it. When I first arrived there in 1946, the town was recovering from the effects of World War II. During that period, the influx of people into military installations increased the population and activities in the otherwise quaint town. Most of them were gone by the time I arrived. The town and the native inhabitants were settling down to their prewar activities and lifestyle.

This town, with unsurpassed beauty, depended directly or indirectly upon maritime activities. Many men put out to sea in old wooden-hulled Nova Scotia–built boats. The gasoline-powered automobile engines they used to power these vessels were noisy. Crossing the hazardous Chatham Bar daily, they ventured far into the Atlantic Ocean. Their fish (such as cod, haddock, and halibut) were sold to the Boston and New York markets upon return. Other men fished from traps located in Nantucket Sound, while still others scratched along the shores for shellfish such as clams, quahogs, and mussels.

Another major contributor to the town was the US Coast Guard. The Chatham lifeboat station and Monomoy Point lookout station required support from the town and local merchants, as did the lightships of Pollock Rip, Stonehorse, and Handkerchief, which maintained stations off the coast. Together, fishermen, coastguardsmen, shopkeepers, doctors, lawyers, ministers, and such were interrelated. They depended on the waters surrounding them for survival.

To understand this relationship, one needs only to stand at the bluff of Chatham. Looking out upon the Atlantic Ocean, the view is endless, broken only by the waters of Old Harbor with the barrier of North Beach in between. The red painted hulls of Pollock Rip and Stonehorse lightships, with bright white letters painted on their sides indicating their names, glisten in the sun. To the south, one can see the white frothing water of waves breaking in the shallows of Chatham Bar, the hazardous passage to the ocean beyond.

Also to the south lie the landmasses of Morris Island and Monomoy Island. They provide a division between the ocean and the waters of Nantucket Sound located on the other side. Turning around, one sees the prominence of Chatham Lighthouse and the Coast Guard lifeboat station. Large sea clamshells painted white are carefully spaced along a hummock of the lawn. They spell out United States Coast Guard Station Chatham.

The Beach Club is alongside, and quaint Cape Cod houses are seen, along with a glimpse of Stage Harbor and Nantucket Sound beyond. This is a very special place surrounded by waters that are interconnected with each other. Chatham could only have been created by the hand of God.

This was the place I came to know. I soon felt that it was under God's direction and control. I felt this way after having observed man had little or no control over the elements, the ever-changing shape of waterfront lands, or the depth of channels, where currents flowed at will.

I would see the tragedy of lives lost at sea and the joy and miracles of lives saved. I would come to know the close association between man and his environment. I would also participate in what can best be explained as the workings of the Lord.

A Boy's Awkward Pursuits

It was 1943, and World War II was in full swing. My dad was serving as associate pastor at Tremont Temple Baptist Church in Boston, Massachusetts. He had come a long way from the little country church in Rowley, and moved on to the larger churches at Avon and Mattapan to reach this large city church.

The business of religion was good. The pews and collection plates were filled at each church service. Radio broadcasts that reached out to those in their homes who were unable to attend services brought even more support for the church and its programs.

My father and mother were happy about many things. Finally, they were a part of a ministry that provided them a decent living. Many new friendships were cultivated and among them were people with great influence and wealth.

However, the war was cause for their concern. Brother Paul left with the first draft and served the Army's Twenty-Sixth Division in Germany. Brother Bob served the US Coast Guard. Brother Bill served the Army Transportation Corps and was off building the Alaskan Highway. Their three sons away from home made them worry. But it was I who worried them the most, I'm sure. I was fifteen at the time. Busy as they were with church activities, it was difficult for them to keep track of my activities and movements. They knew I wasn't what might be called a bad boy, but they also knew I could get into mischief and was easily led. The war mania created an atmosphere that could get a young fellow into trouble.

Dad expressed his concerns about me one day to an influential deacon of the church. The man was president of a steel company and quite wealthy. As a result of that conversation, it was agreed that I should attend Mount Hermon Preparatory School at Greenfield, Massachusetts, and pursue a career in the ministry. Of course, I was not consulted.

My "career" at Mount Hermon was doomed from the beginning. I felt out of place. The deacon paid my tuition, and my father was to pay the other incidental expenses that added up to more than he really could afford.

Wearing my brothers' hand-me-down clothes, with very limited allowance and neither scholastically nor athletically inclined, I wasn't a prime candidate for either Mount Hermon or the ministry. Nevertheless, I plowed along, working in the school laundry, attending classes, and generally trying to understand why I was there.

I had thought about running away from Mount Hermon when a junior-high-school chum named Milton Anderson provided me the added support I needed to follow my thoughts through. Milton had wrecked his father's car one day and had run away himself. He thought of me and decided to come for a visit. His arrival caused me no end of problems. Milton had no money and no place to stay. I felt obligated to hide him out at the school and steal food from the dining room for him to eat. I knew if the authorities found us out, it would be the end of us both.

After a few days, we were caught, and there was hell to pay. Not hanging around for the wrath of the school authorities, we took off through the corn-fields and among the hills surrounding the school and escaped. Eventually, we ended up back home. There was no place else for two fifteen-year-olds to go.

Dad was understandably upset. What to do now with this rebellious son of his? When I turned sixteen years old, I provided him with the answer. I heard about the US Maritime Service and that they were taking sixteen-year-olds for training in New York. Upon completion, I could serve on merchant ships in the war effort. Pleading with my father to let me go, he reluctantly signed the enlistment papers. Many years later, we would talk about this period in my life, and he would say the decision was the work of the Lord and it was the beginning of God's plan for me.

After leaving home, I received training at Sheeps-head Bay Maritime School in New York. There, I learned the fundamentals of seamanship. The highlight of the training experience was meeting the famous prizefighter Jack Dempsey, who was a commander in the Coast Guard and served as the athletic instructor for both the Maritime Service Training Station and the Coast Guard training station located next door at Manhattan Beach.

When the training ended, I was shipped to Panama and placed aboard a merchant ship named SS *Sinclair Rubiline*, which was a T2 tanker. From the ports of Aruba and Curacao in the Caribbean, we carried gasoline to the South Pacific in support of the war effort. This experience would be of prime importance to my life later on.

With the war nearly over, I returned home and enlisted in the US Coast Guard.

The SS Sinclaire Rubiline *as she appeared in 1942 in her wartime garb with 3"-50 and 4"-50 gun mounts bow and stern. There were 20 mm cannons in gun tubs over the pilot house and aft of the stack. Also in use at that period were the old-fashioned square wooden life rafts, mounted fore and aft amidships. (Photo courtesy of the Mariners Museum, Newport News, Virginia.)*

A Transient Visit
Inspiration for a Career

On 26 February 1946, I enlisted in the US Coast Guard. Sent to their training station at Curtis Bay, Maryland, I soon found out this was a very different sea service from what I had previously experienced in the Merchant Marine. The philosophy of the Coast Guard is well explained in the following excerpts from the commanding officer of a Coast Guard training station in his letter to a recruit, which was written on 8 February 1946:

> *I welcome you into the U.S. Coast Guard. It is a tough outfit, proud of its long history of efficient service. It wants only men who are willing and eager to do their best at all times and who have the guts to see a hard job through to the very end.*
>
> *Hard jobs are "routine" in this service. In a way, the Coast Guard is always at war: in wartime, against armed enemies of the nation; and in peacetime, against all enemies of mankind at sea; Fire, Collision, Lawlessness, Gales, Ice, Derelicts, and many more.*

The Coast Guard, therefore, is no place for a quitter, or for a crybaby, or for a four-flusher,* or for anyone who cannot "keep his eye on the ball." Your period of recruit training is a time of test, hour by hour and day by day, to determine whether or not you are made of the right material. It is up to you, as an individual, to prove your worth.

I must have been made of the "right material," because I completed my training. Whether I was to "prove my worth" is a matter for others to judge.

Transferred from Curtis Bay, Maryland, to Cape Cod, I was then assigned to become one of the keepers of Highland Lighthouse at North Truro. I was elated by the assignment and was most fortunate to receive my first duty station close to home. However, duty at Highland was short lived. Six months later, I was to be reassigned to the Gay Head Lighthouse on Martha's Vineyard, located off the coast of Woods Hole, Massachusetts.

Departing Highland Lighthouse on an early October morning, I was transported to Chatham, where I would spend a few days at the Chatham lifeboat station in transit before moving onto Martha's Vineyard Island. It was during this period that I would get to know the town of Chatham, become acquainted with the lifeboat station, and make some personal decisions about my

---

* *The expression "four-flusher" may have different sources. One appears to come from the game of poker. In this regard it refers to a player who only has four of the five game-suit cards required for a "flush."*

future. I felt an attraction to the town of Chatham and sensed that there was a reason I had been brought to this place.

As I arrived in town in the Coast Guard pickup truck, passing Chatham Bars Inn from the truck window, I observed a strange-looking craft moored out in Old Harbor. I caught just a glimpse of her. Just a fleeting glance, only time enough to note the "CG36500" painted in black letters on her bow and the word "Chatham" painted on her stern. At the time, I wasn't particularly impressed.

I asked the driver of the truck what that boat out in the water was. He said it was a thirty-six-foot Coast Guard motor lifeboat. That particular boat in time would become one of the most important factors in my life and the lives of many others.

The Chatham lifeboat station in 1946 was not a very imposing place. The facility consisted of a lighthouse tower located in the front yard. Behind the tower, there was a duplex building that at one time housed the lighthouse keepers and their families. Off to the side was another old foundation for another lighthouse. At one time, there were two lighthouses located on the property, then known as the Twin Lights at Chatham. Several years before, one tower was relocated to Eastham, and this became what is known as Nauset Lighthouse. The remaining foundation was now used to plant flowers.

Several years before, the Coast Guard had abandoned the station on Morris Island. Taking over the

Company "I" at the US Coast Guard training station (boot camp) at Curtis Bay, Maryland, where new coastguardsmen received their basic training prior to assignment to a cutter or station. Bernie Webber is in the last row on the right.

lighthouse property, they proceeded to knock out walls and otherwise make it suitable for the twelve or so men who would be stationed there to operate what would become what is known as the Chatham lifeboat station.

Located behind the main building were two cheaply made wartime structures. One, known as the "Loran shack," housed three men and the equipment required to operate what was called the Loran Monitoring Station. A ninety-foot pole outside provided the antenna for the system, whereby Loran stations at Nantucket and Bodie Island would be checked from Chatham to ensure they were sending out the proper electronic signals. The other building was known as the "motor mack shack." It housed two men and provided work space for the lifeboat station engineers. Space in the rear provided a boatswain locker and storage space.

Another building, located further away from the main building at the lower end of the yard, provided for the Coast Guard telephone men who maintained all the Coast Guard lines that hooked up the stations on Cape Cod. In it was an office and work space, a storage area, and a three-vehicle garage.

The grounds of the Chatham lifeboat station were enclosed by a chain-link fence. Gates at the front and rear provided access onto the property. A wooden walk in front led to the entrance door of the station. The grounds around the property were a considerable area to maintain with non-powered hand mowers. However, the station crew took great pride in the property and kept it neatly mowed. They made improvements in the appearance of the station property by placing stones brought from the shore all along the drives

In 1949, the old Chatham lifeboat station (center) with the Loran shack to the left. The lighthouse is on the right, and the ninety-foot Loran antenna pole can be seen in the center. (Photo by the Author.)

and painting them white. A gully in the front yard provided a banking whereby the crew placed the aforementioned sea clamshells spelling out the words "United States Coast Guard Station Chatham." The painted white shells made the words stand out. Each time the grass was mowed, the shells and stones were moved, then replaced. The crew did all they could to keep the grounds neat and pretty to coincide with the surroundings.

Rescue equipment at the station in 1946 basically consisted of two thirty-six-foot wooden Coast Guard motor lifeboats. They were powered by Sterling Petrel gasoline engines of ninety horsepower. There was also a thirty-eight-foot wooden Coast Guard picketboat powered by a Kermath gasoline engine and a World War II amphibious vehicle, classified as a DUKW.

The station equipment was spread out all around the town, necessary due to the geographical arrangement of the town and surrounding waters. One lifeboat was kept on a mooring out in Old Harbor. The other lifeboat and the picketboat were kept on moorings at Stage Harbor. This was done so that access to the Atlantic Ocean and Nantucket Sound would be readily available under all circumstances. In order to get out to the boats on their moorings, wooden nineteen-foot dories were kept on the beach at both locations. They would be rowed to the moorings and tied there while the powerboats were in use.

The lifeboat-station crew now resided in the old lighthouse keeper's quarters. A room at the front served as a place where a twenty-four-hour watch was maintained. The telephone switchboard and ship-to-shore radio equipment was located there. A coastguardsman on duty answered the phone and radio communications. Every thirty minutes, he was required to make a trip. Out the front door he would go, watchman's clock and binoculars slung over his shoulder, down the wooden walkway to the front of the station, open the gate, then cross the street to a place on the Chatham Bluff where a post contained a key that he would punch in on his watchman's clock, assuring he was awake and at his post. Once there, the man would scan the horizon. Looking offshore, he would take note of all he saw. By day, the lightships, small boats, and larger vessels were obvious, the buoys stood like tin men to his eye. At night, only the lights could be seen. He looked for signs of distress in the area, a fire upon the water, a rocket up in the air, anything out of the ordinary, which indicated trouble.

Returning to the watch office in the station, the man would make an entry in the station log noting his observations. The whole process had to be repeated in thirty minutes. These watches were sometimes difficult during the winter. However, during the summer, the duty was often looked forward to as a means of meeting the local girls that just happened to be strolling by.

Chatham lifeboat station in 1946 was a very busy place. In addition to the rescue work, which was the station's primary duty, the boats were kept on the move in support of three lightships on station offshore. The Pollock, Stonehorse, and Handkerchief lightships depended on the Chatham station to bring groceries and supplies out to them and transfer their personnel. Many other services were also required to keep them operating.

For the twelve or so men assigned to the Chatham station, it meant extreme duty hours. Generally, a crewman spent ten days at the unit, then, if possible, was granted two days off. A crewman was not allowed outside the gates of the station unless on Coast Guard business. The only recreation was to listen to the radio. Even then, its use was regulated. Television was unheard of. It didn't matter whether your wife, mother, God, or anyone else needed you. The Coast Guard had first and last claim on our life, 24 hours a day, 365 days each year. Thoughts of leave, liberty, and the pursuit of happiness had to wait until it suited the Coast Guard.

These lifeboat men of the Coast Guard were true public servants. They were disciplined to stand watch twenty-four hours a day, alert to signs of distress. They maintained the equipment and made, by hand, all possible items needed in order to save taxpayers' money. Further, they knew a distress call required instant response, regardless of the weather. They knew that the Coast Guard motto, "you have to go out, but you don't have to come back," prevailed.

In 1946, the average pay for most of us ranged somewhere between $21.00 and $75.00 per month.[*] A crewman was not allowed to be married until he reached second class petty officer status, and

[*]*One calculation puts this as little as $1,000 per month in 2016 dollars.*

then only with the permission of his commanding officer. A married coastguardsman at the time received medical services only for himself; families were not provided for.

Nevertheless, I, for one, found an attraction to this Chatham station. It was quite different from the duty that I had come from at Highland Lighthouse. I was sorry when I had to move on to my new assignment at Gay Head Lighthouse on Martha's Vineyard Island.

On my way out of town, I saw her once again— the lifeboat CG36500—resting on her mooring in Old Harbor. The boat fascinated me at the time for reasons I couldn't understand. Somehow, I knew I would return to this place.

A Return to Chatham

I returned to Chatham in 1949 after having served three years at Gay Head Lighthouse on Martha's Vineyard Island and aboard Coast Guard cutters on the North Atlantic weather patrol. My orders to Chatham came as no surprise. I knew when I left in 1946 that I would return.

The next four years that I would serve there changed my life dramatically.

As I arrived in Chatham, the town appeared pretty much as I had remembered it: the same quaint place, with a clean atmosphere and neat Cape Cod–style homes. Perhaps there was a new shop or two on Main Street or a few more fishermen working from the fish pier, departing out of Aunt Lydia's Cove and crossing Chatham Bar daily in pursuit of fresh fish. Alton Kenney's boatyard was busy, where he and Elisha Bearse took care of the ills of the fleet. The Sou'wester and Jake's remained as places for blowing off steam. The Dutch Oven on Main Street was available for those who wanted good coffee and conversation.

I was happy to be back until I learned that I would spend the first few days of my return lugging coal from the Old Harbor Coast Guard station located over on North Beach. The station had been abandoned by the Coast Guard. Appropriations tight, it was determined that the tons of coal should be removed and used at the active units. This meant putting the coal in burlap bags, carrying it over the beach, placing it in a dory, and rowing it to the other side. Then it was loaded on trucks for transportation to other Coast Guard units—a backbreaking job.

It was after one of these grueling days of lugging coal that I received my first taste of rescue work. Tired, I had gone to bed early. I was awakened by someone pulling my foot. I was told to get up and to get dressed as I was to be part of a crew to be sent out to a ship that had grounded somewhere off Pollock Rip Channel. Going downstairs, I felt the excitement of the prospect of going out in one of the station's boats. First Class Boatswain's Mate Leo Gracie was to take charge of the thirty-eight-foot picketboat to be sent out to aid the stricken vessel. I had hoped it would be the CG36500 that would be sent. I still yearned for a ride in her.

As I watched Leo get ready to leave the station, gathering up charts and other things he needed for the venture, I couldn't help noticing this man. Older than the rest of us, he cut a dashing figure and had an air of importance about him. He appeared to be proud of his status as an operator of rescue vessels. I decided then and there that I, too, wanted to become one of those boatswain's mates of the Coast Guard that operated rescue vessels.

The Stranding of a Destroyer
USS Livermore

The destroyer USS *Livermore*, with mostly a naval reserve crew on board, was transiting Nantucket Sound. The ship had passed Cross Rip Lightship and was heading down the channel toward the Handkerchief Lightship. Upon arrival at Handkerchief Lightship, a course was then set for Stonehorse Lightship.

It was a clear night, and the sea was calm, with nearly a full moon glistening upon the water. The year was 1949. With the war now over, reservists due for discharge would be going home. The atmosphere on board the old two-piper must have been a happy one; morale should have been high. The crew certainly must have been thinking about their prospects of returning home to loved ones. And to civilian life.

It would appear that the ship and its crew had everything going for them. After all, the channel up ahead was well marked by lightships, with buoys in between, flashing their lights of either white, green, or red, which would show the way for safe passage. It wasn't far to the end of Pollock Rip Channel. Once there, the destroyer in the open sea would be able to pick up speed, which would take them even more rapidly toward port.

The USS *Livermore* moved close by Stonehorse Lightship. Then for some reason, she did not make the necessary course change to the right, which would have taken the ship safely up the Pollock Rip Channel, passing between the buoys with their lights flashing.

Instead, the *Livermore* moved straight ahead and eventually came to a halt. There she rested high and dry on Bearses Shoal, located off Monomoy Island. The ship must have been moving along at a pretty fair clip to land where it did. It was no common feat: She had to pass over two lesser shoals in order to come to a halt where she was now.

Efforts by the crew failed to free the ship from its stranded position. It became necessary for the *Livermore* to report its dilemma. Radio reports were made to naval authorities and the Coast Guard, along with requests for assistance in being freed. For the naval crew, it must have been an embarrassing situation to ask the "Hooligan Navy" (the term used by them when referring to the Coast Guard) for assistance.

Chatham lifeboat station received the call, and preparations were made to render assistance to the *Livermore*. First Class Boatswain's Mate Leo Gracie was ordered to pick a crew and take the station's picketboat out to the scene. I was one of those Gracie selected. This was to be my first experience of going out on a distress call.

For some reason, the thirty-eight-foot Coast Guard picketboat, which was normally kept in Stage Harbor,

USS naval destroyer Livermore, *aground and listing over on Bearses Shoal off Monomoy Point. Tug abow from Boston Navy Yard. (Photo by the Author.)*

was tied up in Old Harbor. This meant Gracie would have to pilot the picketboat out Old Harbor and over Chatham Bar before proceeding down the outside coast to where the *Livermore* lay. At the time, I was amazed at Leo's skill in navigating the channel at night. Fortunately, Chatham Bar was calm. Once clear, we picked up speed and headed south toward the lights, which we knew were coming from the stranded destroyer *Livermore.*

As we arrived near the scene, the destroyer presented an eerie sight. The ship was resting high up on the shoal and was canted over on its side. With a few deck lights burning, the superstructure glowed. It all made for a spectacular sight. Many of the destroyer's crew were lined up along the rails. Some catcalled to us—what did we "hooligans" think we could do for them with the spit-kit we were riding in? Meaning, how could we possibly help the large vessel with our little boat? The same question, I'm sure, crossed Leo Gracie's mind. Nevertheless, we stood alongside the

USS Livermore *aground Bearses Shoal. Boston Navy Yard tug pushes on bow in futile attempt to free the vessel. (Photo by the Author.)*

stricken destroyer in our little picketboat. We knew several large ships were ordered to the *Livermore*'s aid, and in time, we would prove our worth.

We stayed at the scene of the *Livermore* for the remainder of the night. The next morning, ships began to arrive in the area. Tugboats came from Boston naval shipyard, and navy salvage ships arrived from Newport, Rhode Island. The Coast Guard sent its powerful salvage tug *Acushnet*. By midday, an armada had gathered off Monomoy Island.

Preparations were made to free the destroyer *Livermore*. However, due to the shoal waters, the larger vessels were required to remain some distance away. It was necessary to string out heavy hawsers spanning the distance between the *Livermore* and the rescue vessels. We were soon earning our keep. Leo and those of us in the picketboat crew were required to tow the hawsers across the water and get them up aboard the *Livermore*, where they could be secured. The first attempts to free the *Livermore* during a high tide failed, and the heavy hawsers broke under the strain. New hawsers were run out in advance of a coming tide. While awaiting the proper moment, the picketboat crew was kept busy transporting supplies and personnel between the vessels.

Several failed attempts were made. The sailors aboard the destroyer *Livermore* were obviously becoming irritated by their plight. When the picketboat would come alongside with yet another heavy hawser, sometimes apples, oranges, and even steel shackles were hurled at us, along with a few choice words not in the nature of a compliment. We understood though, sailors are a strange lot and act in odd ways in a given situation.

Soon their predicament was over. During a high tide, with the combined efforts of the large salvage tugs pulling together along with the smaller tugs pushing up against the destroyer *Livermore*, she began to move and was freed from the shoal and floating in deep water again. A cheer went up from the *Livermore*'s crew. Whistles blew from the rescue vessels standing by.

It was not long before the *Livermore* was underway with the convoy of ships escorting her. As the armada went down over the horizon, Leo Gracie and his picketboat headed into Chatham over the sandbars.

The only explanation for the incident was that the destroyer USS *Livermore* mistook Chatham Lighthouse that particular night for Pollock Rip Lightship. The excuse appears to be as shallow as the water into which the *Livermore* ventured, since each light showed a very different characteristic and would bear in a different compass direction.

First Assignments at Chatham
Loran Unit and Monomoy Lookout Station

Once having had a taste of rescue work during the *Livermore* incident, I was very disappointed when I was assigned to supervise the Loran unit at Chatham life-boat station. I was a coxswain at the time, and the billet called for a lower rating, so I fitted the need.

For me, the unit was boring duty. There were three of us assigned to the unit, Edmund Paul, Bob McDonald, and myself. Usually, one or the other of us was on leave or liberty. The remaining two would stand watch—six hours on, then six hours off. In a room totally painted black, with no lights on, we observed Loran scopes that showed electronic signals coming from Nantucket and Bodie islands. It was up to us to monitor the signals and ensure they were transmitting property. It was not a very exciting job.

Fortunately, a couple of months later I was reassigned to the Monomoy Point lookout station as the supervisor of a subunit of Chatham lifeboat station. Again, I was disappointed at not receiving an assignment to the regular lifeboat-station crew, yet I rejoiced at getting away from the "black room."

Monomoy Island was a fascinating place. The bare natural terrain, full of wildlife, created an atmosphere of special beauty. The Coast Guard lookout station at the point of Monomoy was several miles from the mainland. It was isolated by two bodies of water. Reaching the station was at times difficult. A cut-through of water separated mainland Chatham from Morris Island. A second cut-through to the south divided Morris Island from Monomoy. In order to get to Monomoy from Chatham, it was first necessary to row a dory across Stage Harbor, more often than not with groceries and supplies. On Morris Island, a jeep was available for the trip down the beach or over the dunes to the station. However, the cut-through to the south of Morris Island had to be crossed in the vehicle. The jeep would be driven through the shallow water, evading deeper holes eaten out by the current flowing through. Any crossing had to be made during low tides. Often, storms, which kept the tides high, made crossing impossible, in which case we would be stranded sometimes for days on one side or the other.

There were only three coastguardsmen assigned to Monomoy Point lookout station: Seaman Larry Samuelson, Seaman Harold Glaskow, and me, who, as a coxswain, was in charge of supervising the place. I soon found out it was a zoo full of people. At the time, besides coastguardsmen, there were several air force personnel residing at the station. They maintained an air force bombing range on Monomoy about halfway up the island from the point. Planes from Otis Air Force Base at Falmouth flew almost daily over Monomoy and bombed or strafed the range.

Seaman Robert Doman (in bow) and Seaman Walter Coates (aft) in Coast Guard fourteen-foot dory, making a landing on Morris Island after rowing across Stage Harbor. Note: Jeep in background used for transportation to Monomoy Point in 1949. (Photo by the Author.)

The air force personnel had it made. We coast guards, as their hosts, maintained the station, keeping it clean, and kept the generator and thirty-two-volt battery electrical system in operation as well as the water pump. We lugged the coal and kept the cranky cookstove in the galley operating for them. We also were required to maintain a twenty-four-hour-a-day lookout watch from the station tower. It seemed to us that all those air force boys had to do was live at the station and play.

With just our jeep for transportation, we coast guards were often stranded at high tides and by stormy weather. The air force personnel were furnished with an amphibious vehicle called a DUKW. This allowed them the freedom of coming and going up and down the beach between the mainland and Monomoy Point as they desired. They were a wild bunch. Often they would arrive at their station with a DUKW full of giggling girls and plenty of beer, ready to have a party. For those of us in the Coast Guard, it was at times a problem. We were under strict discipline. Not that we

View from roof of Monomoy station equipment building. Below are fish shanties and cottages around Powder Hole Pond. (Photo by the Author.)

didn't join in a party or two. It was just necessary that we keep the lid on, so as not to get caught.

Most of the air force boys had served during the war on some pretty tough duty. Monomoy gave them a place with the freedom to blow off steam, and they were making the most of it. Soon, many were due for discharge and return to civilian life.

Supposedly, they were to maintain checkpoints at each end of the bombing range. Their job was to prevent anyone from straying into the line of fire from the air force planes that bombed and strafed the place. It was not necessary for them to man the place when the range wasn't being used. However, as I found out one day, perhaps they didn't think it necessary that anyone be stationed at the checkpoints at any time due to the isolation of Monomoy.

One particular day, I was returning to Monomoy

Point after shopping for groceries at Chatham. Arriving at the checkpoint prior to entering the range, I found it unattended. Assuming there were no practice runs being made that day, I proceeded to drive on through. When about halfway across the range in the jeep, I heard the roar of an airplane engine, followed by the sound of guns rapidly firing. Then suddenly in front of me, puffs of sand spurted up in the air.

Stopping the jeep, I immediately crawled underneath, just as a plane swooped overhead. When I knew it has passed, I peeked out from my position in time to see the plane turning around to the east, heading out over the ocean. I then crawled out from under the jeep, thanking God the pilot of the plane must have realized his mistake.

I no sooner had the thought than I watched the plane continue its turn and head right back toward me again. I again dove for cover under the jeep, anticipating what was about to happen. On came the plane, as before, and strafed the area. After it passed this time, I got in the jeep and drove like hell to get out of there. As I was driving along over the dunes, I saw the plane again, only this time it was beside me at eye level, not thirty feet off the ground. I swear I could see a grin on the pilot's face as he went by, wagging the plane's wings. Later, I found out that the airman who was to be guarding the checkpoint was too busy catching a thirty-five-pound bass from the nearby beach.

Not long after the incident with the plane on the bombing range, the Stonehorse Lightship, which was anchored on station about a half mile off the beach at the point of Monomoy, also experienced one of the air force's finest. The ship was strafed in a similar manner. Fortunately, nobody was hurt, and the ship received little damage, only minor scars.

Later on, the bombing range was closed. We said our goodbyes to our air force friends. It had been an experience. We three coastguardsmen now had Monomoy to ourselves. The place seemed empty to us, especially when one man was off the island on liberty and another was in town on business, occasionally stranded for days. For the man left alone at the Monomoy Point station, it was a lonesome, if not scary, experience. The old building creaked and groaned in the wind, and one would swear he heard voices and footsteps, thinking perhaps they came from the ghosts of old surf men that had served at Monomoy long ago.

Our days were spent keeping the station operating and standing the required lookout-tower watches.

Monomoy station, 1949. (Photo by the Author.)

Seaman Larry Samuelson sits on Coast Guard jeep. Coxswain Bernie Webber in jeep, holding "Jeff" at Monomoy station. (Photo from the Author's collection.)

Occasionally, something would happen that livened things up. It didn't take much. One day, a sixty-foot whale came ashore on the beach in front of the station. The commanding officer of the Chatham lifeboat station, Alvin Newcomb, and some his men arrived at the point in one of the station's motor lifeboats to tow it off to sea. Otherwise, our fun or diversion from the monotony and isolation at Monomoy was found in digging clams from the Powder Hole, a small saltwater pond located behind the station. We also trapped muskrats in the area. We skinned them out, stretched them on a board to dry, then sometimes sold them to Sears Roebuck Company, receiving as much as $1.50 for a pelt. Occasionally, we could catch a bass from the beach.

We washed our clothes by hand in a bucket of rainwater, cooked for ourselves, and generally survived on our own. The duty did provide a freedom unlike any other Coast Guard assignment. I was able to bring my dog, a black cocker spaniel named Jeff, down to Monomoy Point to live with us. He became a member of our little Coast Guard family. Jeff and I together would roam the island by day and chase the foxes at Monomoy Point in our jeep at night. I think Jeff thought he was in heaven, eating what we ate, riding in the jeep, and chasing the plentiful wildlife at the point. His days were filled with enjoyment. I knew that, for him, it beat being back in Milton, tied up, with only an occasional pat on the head.

Duty at Monomoy Point lookout station came to an abrupt end. One day, we were ordered to close the station—to pack everything up and come to the Chatham lifeboat station. We had mixed feelings about leaving Monomoy. With winter coming on, we felt a relief. However, we also knew that we would never again have such freedom in the service. But it would be good to be around more people, and at a station where there was a cook, and generally back in the mainstream of Coast Guard activity.

A Desire Finally Realized

With the closing of Monomoy Point lookout station, I finally realized my desire to be assigned to the regular crew of the Chatham lifeboat station. It meant that, as coxswain, I would finally have the opportunity to operate Coast Guard boats and to perform other duties my rating called for. I would be able to participate and feel some of the excitement of rescue work and come to realize it sometimes meant danger and required one to put his life on the line. In time, I would learn what being a lifeboat man meant.

At the lifeboat station in 1949, there was a kind old-timer in charge by the name of Alvin E. Newcomb. His rank was that of a chief warrant officer boatswain. He would retire in the near future with nearly thirty years of Coast Guard service. We affectionately referred to him as Mother Newcomb for several reasons. His only child was a daughter. As a result, his crew at the station became adopted sons. We all grew to love this man because of his concern for us and our well-being. He wanted to know our whereabouts at all times, not only to ensure that we hadn't sneaked away from the station by taking a little unauthorized liberty, but to ensure we were available in the event of an emergency. Also, he didn't want any of us to get into trouble.

At night, Alvin Newcomb would make bed checks on his crew and roam the station yard with a flashlight in hand. Smoking the pipe that was forever in his mouth, his presence was announced long before his arrival. I think he planned it that way so as not to catch any of the crew that might be lurking around the station yard, in the dark, with some of the local girls. I especially developed respect and affection for this man, so much so that I gave him my dog, Jeff. I was unable to keep Jeff at the station and knew the dog had grown fond of Cape Cod. For Alvin Newcomb, the dog truly became a son. They were the best of pals, and the dog wanted for nothing.

Another key figure at the Chatham lifeboat station during this period was Alvin Newcomb's assistant, Frank Masachi. Frank was another Coast Guard old-timer, a burly chief boatswain's mate who had weathered many a storm. Alvin Newcomb depended on Frank to keep the station crew in line and generally run the place. A crusty old salt, Frank was tough. However, the crew found his soft spots and looked up to him with great respect.

Regardless of the rank or position that these two men held, or the fact that they lived but a stone's throw away from the station in the town of Chatham, they were rarely allowed to be at home with their families. They spent their ten days at a time aboard with the rest of us. Often, I would see Frank's kids hanging around

Some of the Chatham lifeboat station crew on Thanksgiving Day, 1950. Left to right, standing: Seaman Edward Massey, Seaman Robert McGrath, Engineman Third Class Richard Chillson, Coxswain Bernard Webber, Seaman Edmund Paul. Sitting: Engineman Stan Dauphinais, Robert Doman. (Photo from the Author's collection.)

out by the front gate, hoping to see their dad and perhaps talk with him for a minute. During these days, we all were married to the Coast Guard, which meant duty, duty, duty first. All other things came second, if at all.

The other men at the station, with names like Stan Dauphinais, Ed Massey, Mel Gouthro, Walter Coates, and Mahlon Chase, were either seamen, cooks, engineers, or whatever, who made the place operate. Some were native Cape Codders; others were from many parts of the United States. All were required to be dedicated to the Coast Guard and to the community of Chatham that they served.

Some of the station's crew with handmade fenders (bumpers) for use on station boats. (Photo by the Author.)

We really were a Coast Guard family at Chatham lifeboat station. There were formalities. For example, at mealtimes, the crew would gather around the long dining table and stand until the man in charge, Alvin Newcomb, arrived. Then we would all be seated together. Frank Masachi would sit to the right of Newcomb, the others sat along the table according to rank. At times, it was unfortunate for the lower-ranked men, as sitting down at the far end of the table meant the choice items of food would have already been taken.

There was respect and protocol, and our lives were disciplined. The system not only kept us organized, it provided security and stabilization in our young lives.

Soon, I would begin to experience the true work of a Coast Guard lifeboat station. I would go through a series of events that seemed to provide a period of development and training in a direction that would be very much needed during my future Coast Guard service.

The Night the Landry Went Down

7 April 1950. A wild nor'easter blowing off Cape Cod. Winds seventy-plus miles per hour with snow, sleet, and heavy seas. In the blackness of the night, the captain of the fishing dragger *William J. Landry* fought to keep his vessel on course toward Pollock Rip Lightship. His boat was floundering. He was alone in the pilothouse while his crew below bailed for their lives, trying to keep up with the water coming in through the seams of the old wooden-hulled vessel.

The *Landry* had already sent out a radio distress call. The message was received by Pollock Rip Lightship and further relayed to the Chatham lifeboat station. Guy V. Emro, the lightship skipper, spoke with Alvin E. Newcomb, the officer in charge at the Chatham station, about the *Landry*'s plight. Between them, plans were made to assist the fishing vessel. Chatham was to dispatch a motor lifeboat offshore to the aid of the *Landry*. Pollock Lightship was to make ready a hawser to send over to the fishing vessel in the event it was able to reach the lightship ahead of the lifeboat's arrival. The idea was that once the fishing vessel made fast astern of the lightship, perhaps portable pumps could be sent aboard to control the flooding.

Unfortunately, none of the plans worked out. The *Landry* was able to make it to the Pollock Lightship but never did take the lightship's hawser. The motor lifeboat from Chatham did not get out of Chatham that night. As a result, the *Landry* sank, with loss of all hands on board. Many questions were raised. The public wanted to know why rescue attempts had failed. Subsequently, an investigation was conducted. It was held at the Chatham lifeboat station. High-ranking Coast Guard officers were sent from Boston headquarters to investigate and determine why the Chatham crew failed in getting a lifeboat to the *Landry*'s assistance that night.

To this day, there are those who question the *Landry*'s sinking and loss of its entire crew. As a member of that Chatham crew, here is what happened: Although a public explanation was given by Coast Guard authorities at the time, it didn't capture the facts or details of the human efforts made that night.

Nothing in my entire Coast Guard career that followed made such an impression on me as the loss of the fishing vessel *William J. Landry*—not only the death of the men aboard, but how it affected those of us who were involved at the time.

Aboard the Pollock Rip Lightship, Chief Warrant Officer Guy V. Emro ordered Chief Boatswain's Mate Roy Dean and his men to break out a large hawser from down below and lay it out on the lightship's weather decks in preparation for the arrival of the fishing vessel *William J. Landry*. It was hoped that the fishing vessel, upon arrival at the lightship's position, would be able to take the hawser on board, tie it off to the vessel's bows, and lay astern to await the arrival of Chatham's lifeboat.

Pollock Lightship was pitching and rolling in the blackness of breaking seas, snow, and sleet of this early spring northeast gale. As the seas broke over the bows, the ship jerked each time and came up taut on her anchor chain. Dean and his men struggled in the sea spray mixed with snow and sleet on the dimly lit, ice-ridden decks. One man nearly washed over the side, only to be caught by a fellow seaman.

Meanwhile, at Chatham lifeboat station, Chief Warrant Officer Alvin E. Newcomb, with Chief Boatswain's Mate Frank Masachi, formulated plans to aid the stricken fishing vessel. They decided to use the motor lifeboat 36383 and that Frank would skipper it. Frank chose for his crew Melvin F. Gouthro, Antonio Ballerini, and me. The lifeboat 36383 was kept out on a mooring in Stage Harbor. To reach it, a heavy, wooden, nineteen-foot dory had to be launched from a nearby beach and rowed out to the lifeboat on its mooring.

It is necessary to mention that another lifeboat was available at Old Harbor, Chatham: the CG36500. This lifeboat was much closer to the scene. However, the thought of using it meant crossing the hazardous Chatham Bar with little opportunity of success in reaching the open sea, much less in making it out to the *Landry*. Although departing from Stage Harbor meant a longer passage, the 36383 from Stage Harbor presented the best means of getting out to sea that night. The decision was made.

Frank Masachi and his lifeboat crew arrived at Stage Harbor. It was necessary to brush the snow off the wooden dory, roll it over to the upright position, install the thole pins, and make the oars ready before dragging it down the beach to the water's edge. Stage Harbor was a frothing mass of white water churned by the high winds. The spitting snow and sleet cut into one's hands and face, and wet clothing through to the bone. Already, the men felt the effects of the weather.

Once made ready, the dory was hauled and pushed down to the water's edge, then further out into the water, the bow afloat. Ballerini stood knee deep in the water, holding the bow steady while Gouthro and I got aboard and took our place at the oars. Frank, at the stern, pushed the boat off and jumped aboard. Ballerini hopped aboard at the bow; both men sat low in the boat. Gouthro and I heaved on the oars, nearly breaking under the strain of our efforts.

Once clear of the beach, heading for the 36383 on its mooring, the dory shipped water over the bows. The two seated men began to bail. The oarsmen struggled to make slow headway.

For the men at the oars, it seemed like an eternity before the dory reached the side of the lifeboat, which was bobbing up and down on its mooring. Their arms ached in their sockets from the strain of rowing. Eager hands reached out to grab ahold of the lifelines that were secured on the sides of the lifeboat. Then it happened. The shift of weight combined with the sea caused the dory to capsize, throwing the men into the water. In a state of shock from being plunged into the icy water, instinctively the four men grabbed ahold of the bottom of the overturned boat and kicked off their boots, now full and heavy with water. Bare-headed, knit caps washed from their heads, soaked clear through their long johns, and adrift in the night. For each, it would have been easy now to drift off into endless sleep, but not these men. They hung on until the dory, pushed along by the wind and sea, beached itself out on Morris Island across from Stage Harbor.

Relieved in making it to shore where they knew shelter could be found in the old boathouse on the otherwise deserted island, the crew thought they would head immediately for the old boathouse in order to get in and out of the wind and weather. Their leader, Frank Masachi, had other ideas. The crusty old seaman, undaunted by the experience, was now ordering us to right the dory, search the beach for the oars, and make ready to try again. Reluctantly, we obeyed. The oars were found further down the beach. The dory was righted and otherwise made ready for another attempt to row out to the 36383.

We had dragged the nineteen-foot boat up the beach about two hundred yards into the wind to a vantage point where we could launch and have a down-sea row to the lifeboat on its mooring. At this point, the effort paid off. Warmed somewhat by the work involved, scared at knowing Frank was determined to try again, all thoughts of our personal discomfort vanished.

A second attempt was made. This time, in the strug-gle of reaching the lifeboat, the thole pins, which hold the oars in place for rowing, broke under the strain, causing the dory to veer and capsize again.

The devastation of our minds and bodies seemed imminent—floundering once again in the icy Stage Harbor waters. However, as before, we made it to the beach, hanging on to the overturned dory.

This time, Frank relented and agreed we should seek shelter in the old boathouse. By no means had Frank given up his attempt to get out to the sinking fishing vessel.

At the boathouse, we kicked in the door for the want of a key. Once inside, we were able to get the old Kohler gasoline-powered generator started and at least had light. What a pitiful sight we were, ravaged by the exposure we had been through. Wasting no time, Frank cranked the old magneto telephone connected to a switchboard at Chatham station on the mainland. Talking with Alvin Newcomb, he learned the fishing vessel *William J. Landry* was still afloat and close by Pollock Lightship. Flooding continued aboard the fishing vessel, which was in dire need of assistance. He explained our situation to Alvin Newcomb and we heard Frank say we were going to try again. Each of us, I'm sure, felt a sickness in the pit of the stomach, not expecting to go out into the elements again.

Before we could think too much about it, Frank had us jumping again. Soon we were cutting up broom handles, whittling them down to replace the thole pins broken in our last attempt. This accomplished, Frank shut down the generator and ordered us out once again into the blackness of the stormy night.

Outside, we made our way down the beach to the dory. Again, an effort was made to reach the lifeboat 36383. Again, the effort failed. This time, the oars broke. We knew then, while drifting in the icy water, hanging on to the overturned dory, that we were finished in our attempts that night. As before, somehow we all made it to the beach, once again washed ashore on Morris Island. We gathered in the boathouse, a frozen, beaten lot. Frank talked with Alvin Newcomb, and they reached a decision that we walk nearly a mile along the Morris Island each to a point where a cut-through channel separated Chatham from the island. It was hoped we might be able to just wade across as the tide was nearing low. Alvin Newcomb was to be on the other side in the station jeep with its lights on to guide us across.

The trek from the boathouse was long and painful for all of us. Some were barefoot, all were bare-headed, soaked through, and frozen to the bone. The thought of reaching the mainland station with its warmth and comfort prodded us on.

After a time, we reached the cut-through. The lights from the jeep on the other side and the shadow of a man we knew was Alvin Newcomb guided us into the waters, which oddly enough seemed warm at this point. The current was swift and the bottom of the cut-through was humpy, making it difficult to walk through the water and maintain balance. It soon became evident the depth was too great for Frank Masachi and Antonio Ballerini, the shorter of the men. It was already up to the necks of Mel Gouthro and me, who were out in front. As it was, it became necessary for the taller men to carry the shorter across, lifting them by their armpits. Two trips were made successfully. Once in the jeep, we were on our way to the Chatham station and the warmth and dry clothing our bodies now cried out for.

During the ride to the station, the only conversation was between Alvin Newcomb and Frank. They were discussing the possibility of using the lifeboat 36500 to go out to the *Landry*. Frank, much older than the rest of us, was willing to give it a try. To us younger men, it was difficult for us to understand how he could think such thoughts, knowing how we had already suffered. We had yet to be warmed and change to dry clothing. Our bodies were wracked by the experience. Frank, I'm sure, took our failure up to this point personally and was determined to follow through in aiding the *Landry* even if it meant our lives in the try.

As we arrived at the station and entered the watch room, the radio crackled. The fishing vessel *William J. Landry* was calling the Pollock Rip Lightship. The Captain on the *Landry* reported his vessel was about a half a mile away from the lightship's position and water was coming in faster than his crew could keep up with. The skipper on Pollock, Guy Emro, told him all was ready aboard the lightship to pass *Landry* a hawser when close enough and that a portable pump was standing by, ready to be passed aboard. As the *Landry* approached, the storm grew more intense.

We had changed clothes and warmed up a bit and were now ready to head down to Old Harbor to man the motor lifeboat CG36500 in a last-ditch effort to get out of Chatham that night to aid the stricken fishing vessel. Over the radio now came the excited voice of the *Landry*'s skipper reporting that during the attempt to retrieve the hawser from the stern of the lightship, the seas brought the two vessels together. The *Landry* was damaged and was taking on even more water. Its crew had difficulty hanging on and now were worn out from the ordeal of the past twenty-four hours. He indicated they would make no further attempt at tying up to the lightship. They would just continue to stand by close to the lightship and await the arrival of the lifeboat from Chatham. Captain Emro on Pollack replied that he understood and, further, that he would keep the lightship's searchlight on the little fishing vessel. No sooner had he said it than over the radio came the words "Oh My God," then all went quite.

From Chatham, Alvin Newcomb called Pollock over the radio. There was no answer at first, then a shaken voice, that of Emro aboard the lightship, replied, reporting that a huge sea, unlike any other, hit the vessel and spun it completely around. However, he still had the *Landry* in view.

No sooner had he said it than the *Landry*'s captain came over the radio and reported that the last sea had finished them. They were taking on much more water than the crew could keep up with, and the engine room was now flooding. His last reply was, "we're going down below to pray and get something to eat. If we die out here it will be with full stomachs, so long, thank you. God bless you all."

Emro, on the lightship, replied that he understood and, further, "God be with you."

It was only moments later that Captain Emro called Chatham station, reporting that the seas had worsened. In the glare from the lightship's searchlight, he had observed the fishing vessel *William J. Landry* go down, taking its crew with it into the black depths of storm-tossed seas.

At Chatham, in the watch room, there was stunned silence. Four bedraggled men stood quiet, heads down staring at the floor. Their bodies still felt the pain and weariness of their earlier attempt to assist the *Landry*. Added now to their burden was a deep ache in their hearts.

• • •

Depression set in at Chatham lifeboat station as a result of this incident. High-ranking officers arrived from Coast Guard headquarters in Boston to make an inquiry. This didn't relieve the atmosphere.

Captain Emro was brought ashore from Pollock Rip Lightship for the occasion. Alvin Newcomb, as the officer in charge of Chatham lifeboat station, Frank Masachi, and those of us who made up his crew in the Stage Harbor attempts that night when the *Landry* sank were all called to testify. We were all questioned and cross-questioned many times. The investigating officers were neither kind nor friendly in their pursuit of the facts. Accusations were made, and it appeared they were intent to place blame for the loss of the *Landry*.

Emro, Newcomb, and Masachi were allowed to remain in the investigation room when we lower-ranked men were called in to give our version of the attempts made that night. They sat quietly, listening to the questions and testimony. As the investigation continued, it was becoming obvious that Frank and his crew were about to be chastised by the investigators. It seemed they couldn't understand the reasoning for our not being able to get to the lifeboat CG36383 the night the *Landry* sank.

Oddly enough, I think we all understood their feelings. After all, they had come down from Boston several days after the incident. It was one of those lovely bright, warm sunny days of spring when the world seems right. Viewing a calm, beautiful Stage Harbor with the little lifeboat CG36383 sitting prettily on its mooring, it was difficult for anyone to comprehend the prevailing conditions of just a few nights before. The snow had melted. It seemed there was no way of making the investigation board believe the very different picture we painted of the occasion when the *Landry* went down. Also, those of us who were involved were now rested from the experience. We were dressed in clean clothes and generally shipshape for this occasion, appearing no worse from our rugged experience.

As the inquiry moved on, it was Captain Emro who rose to the occasion. He stopped the proceedings with a "God damn it! Who do you think you are?" This was directed at the investigating officers. Emro went on to relate the stormy conditions at Pollock Rip Lightship that night. A pin could be heard to drop as he spoke with authority. His crusty bearing developed by thirty years at sea and his old uniform with its brass buttons turned green from sea spray made an impression on the board that could be easily seen by those of us present.

Alvin Newcomb went on to tell of the concentrated effort Frank and his crew made and the risks and exposure they faced—all points these men had failed to mention, being too timid to talk about themselves.

Additionally, a report from the Coast Guard cutter *Hornbeam*, which had been dispatched to the aid of the *Landry* that night, reaffirmed the conditions. It had reported great difficulty of its own during the storm.

The Board of Investigation officers completed their work at Chatham lifeboat station. With nothing but a goodbye, we heard no more from them. We never knew the results of their findings. By us, outwardly, the *Landry* was never mentioned again. But I know each one of us often thought about the little vessel and its crew and felt a special sensation each time we were in the waters around the Pollock Rip.

Fishing Vessel Cachalot
Pitchpoled over Chatham Bar

For the fishermen of Chatham, undoubtedly nothing endangered their lives more than the daily crossing of the bars while going to and coming from the offshore fishing grounds. The Chatham bars encompassed the opening to the Old Harbor.

The bars were treacherous to navigate. Shoals were everywhere. The locations of these shoals constantly changed as a result of the tides running through the opening and the waves that almost constantly ran over and broke upon the shallows. From the deep ocean waters offshore, the swells would come and build to great height as they ran into the shallower water of the bar. Once there, they curled into breakers and gained momentum, racing forward in a foaming mass of power until they finally flattened out upon reaching inside Old Harbor.

Chatham fishermen left the fish pier each day long before the sun came up. They would proceed out over the bar, heading into the sea in their little wooden Novi boats. It was a dangerous venture. Some boats received smashed windshields as a result of running into the waves, others had their cabins ripped off, while yet others became swamped and lay where a huge breaking mass of salt water filled their vessels.

For those who made it safely out to sea for a good day's fishing, they had to face crossing the bar with their boats on a return trip, only now they would have their stern to the sea and would be heavy as a result of the day's catch. This presented an even more dangerous challenge to man and his boat.

The fishermen who made it in over the bar then sold their catch. They were able to provide for and feed their families, and lived to fish another day.

For the fisherman whose boat didn't make it over the bar, it meant almost certain death. There were rare cases however, in which a fisherman, by some fluke, miracle, or act of God, escaped the usual fate and would live after losing his boat out from under him. After having experienced the wrath of Chatham Bar once, they never returned to fish again.

The worst thing that could happen to a fisherman coming in over Chatham Bar with his boat at the end of a day of fishing offshore was to be "pitchpoled" by breakers. The power in the waves would pick a fishing vessel up by the stern and turn it end for end, over and over, sometimes several times, until it landed on the beach in the harbor upside down. For fishermen caught in this situation, it meant certain death.

This was the case of the fishing vessel *Cachalot*. It

was my first experience with such a situation and the first time I came in contact with those who had died as a result of the power of Chatham Bar.

The date was 30 October 1950. Chatham fishermen Archie Nickerson and his partner, Elroy Larkin, had gone out that morning to fish offshore. It was a beautiful day. The sun shone bright and the water glistened in its rays. There was a swell running off the coast. In the clean, clear, Cape Cod air, typical of October, nothing seemed out of place. However, the tide in Old Harbor started to run out. Seas were building and breaking higher on the bar as time went on.

Many of the Chatham fishing fleet had already come in over the bar and entered the harbor. Archie Nickerson and Elroy Larkin in the forty-foot Novi boat approached the bar and started in over it. Suddenly their boat, the *Cachalot,* was picked up by one of the great seas breaking on Chatham Bar, turned end for end and pitchpoled over the bar. It landed on the beach upside down, below Morris Island, in Old Harbor.

At the Chatham lifeboat station, we received word of the incident over the radio from a fisherman in another boat close by who had witnessed the tragedy. Chief Frank Masachi, Stan Dauphinais, and I departed the station immediately and drove down to the Chatham Fish Pier. Once there, we went aboard the Coast Guard motor lifeboat CG36500 and proceeded out Old Harbor to the scene. While en route, we received a radio call from Louis DeEntremont, the captain of the fishing vessel *Carl-Marie.* He informed us that he had located a body floating in the water. He had moved his fishing boat up close to the body and his crew had grabbed it and was hanging on with a boat hook. Louis asked that the CG36500 proceed to him and take the body aboard the lifeboat. Many fishermen have superstitions about dead bodies found at sea. We of the Coast Guard could not think about such things.

The CG36500 arrived alongside Louis DeEntremont's fishing boat. Stan Dauphinais and I grabbed ahold of the drowned body with a boat hook and pulled it up to the side of the lifeboat. We then reached out and tried to pull the victim aboard. Although the man was not large, his weight, under the circumstances, was more than Stan and I could handle. It took all three of us onboard the lifeboat to pull the man aboard. Once we had him, we realized it was Elroy Larkin. The experience was a traumatic one for those of us onboard CG36500. It hit close to home, as we knew these men.

The body of Archie Nickerson was never recovered. His gravestone at Chatham is marked "Lost at Sea." However, the forty-foot boat *Cachalot*, in which Archie Nickerson and Elroy Larkin lost their lives, lived to fish again. It was righted from the beach where it lay after the tragedy, brought in, and rebuilt. It continued to sail for some fifteen years and finally came to a resting place—sunk not three hundred yards from where Archie Nickerson and Elroy Larkin had lost their lives fifteen years before.

Archie Nickerson had a daughter named Beverly. In time, she married a coastguardsman by the name of Richard Livesey, who won a Gold Lifesaving Medal while in service at Chatham lifeboat station.

Elroy Larkin had a son, Murray, and a daughter, Esther. Murray would join the Coast Guard and serve later with Frank Masachi and me on a Coast Guard cutter CG83388 out of Woods Hole, Massachusetts.

Esther Larkin later married Fred Wharenburger, who was the cook at the Chatham lifeboat station.

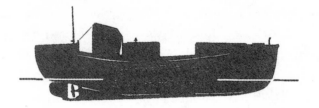

A Car, a Wife, and "Silver Heels"

Duty on a Coast Guard lifeboat station was a growing experience. Life took on a different perspective for young men as they dealt with life-and-death situations. They matured, learned to respect the elements, and recognized their potential for dealing with realities. Although they aged in some ways, a youthfulness was retained by these men, and they pursued other aspects of life in a normal manner.

In 1950, I had been at Chatham for nearly two years. Still a skinny kid with no special skills, I recognized that the Coast Guard provided a purpose in my life and much more. The service fed me, clothed me, and gave me the opportunity to advance. In turn, all that was asked of me was to be honest, do my duty, obey regulations, and be a good public servant. It was just the place for an individual like me, and I was now dedicated.

My father recognized my development. This became obvious to me on one of my rare trips home for a visit to Milton, Massachusetts. Dad indicated that perhaps if I had an automobile for transportation, I would be able to visit home more often. I jumped at his idea but wondered how I could possibly pay for an automobile on my meager service pay. Dad came through. He had connections with a local dealer that attended his church. Arrangements were made for me to buy a 1939 Plymouth two-door sedan. This was a big boost for me, as few men in my situation had a car during these particular days. I was proud of that car. It gave me mobility I never had before. Occasionally, I made it home when I had a day or two off from duty. But, more often than not, it allowed me and others in the Chatham crew to cruise Cape Cod, seeking new horizons in our limited social lives.

One place that we were drawn to was Provincetown, at the tip of Cape Cod. Coastguardsmen seemed to have a special attraction for the local girls. Also, the local pubs and establishments catered to a sailor's image, unlike those in Chatham.

It was on one such excursion to Provincetown that unusual circumstances led to my meeting the girl who later became my wife. It was a rare occasion when three of us from the station could be off duty on the same night. It did happen though, and one night, with two others, we all took off in the old Plymouth. We were headed for Provincetown to date some of the town's lovelies. We made it as far as Orleans when the car broke down after throwing a rod in the engine. I then made a telephone call to Provincetown and informed my date about the mishap and explained the reasons we wouldn't be able to make it that night. At that time, I had no idea that this particular phone call would forever change my life. We had the car towed back to Chatham, and I thought no more about it.

A couple of nights after the incident with my car, Chatham lifeboat station received a telephone call asking for a fellow by the name of Webb. The man on watch came and got me, as my name at least came close. I answered the phone and found myself talking with a young lady who wouldn't tell me her name or anything about herself. All she would say was she had seen me and knew who I was. As we chitchatted, every once in a while she would say over the phone, "wait a sec." I would hear a click, then she would return to talk some more. I thought the whole situation strange and finally told her I had to go. Before she hung up, she asked me if she could call again. I thought about it for a moment and told her to call me when I was on watch, thinking at the time that a call would at least pass the hours away for me when I was alone on duty.

As it turned out, the young lady called several times. Our conversations became longer and longer. However, they were filled with those "wait a sec's." Eventually, I found out why. She was a telephone operator on a switchboard in Wellfleet. This was the reason for the many interruptions. As time went on, I learned she was also a blonde and apparently had other features that livened my interest. I was hooked. I had to meet this girl. I asked her over the phone for a date. She put me off time and again. Finally, I told her either I had to meet her or she shouldn't call me again. Up to this point, the girl really didn't know who I was or what I looked like. It all goes back to the night my car broke down on the way to Provincetown. When I made the telephone call to inform the girls that we wouldn't be able to make it down, this girl, located in the Wellfleet office of the phone company, handled it. She heard me mention the name Webb. As a result, telephone operators being what they were, and Cape Cod girls being where they were, on a lark she decided to call the Coast Guard station, ask for Webb, and see what would happen.

The young lady finally relented and agreed to our having a date—but only under certain circumstances. It would have to be a double date. I would have to bring a friend for her girlfriend. Arrangements were made, and we were to meet in Bob Murray's Drugstore, located on Wellfleet's Main Street. Taking a buddy of mine, Mel Gouthro, along, I headed for Wellfleet on a cold January evening. Arriving in town, we parked in front of the drugstore and went in. There was a girl behind the soda counter by the name of Catherine Paine. Another girl was sitting on a stool. As she didn't meet the description of my date, I asked Catherine if she had seen the girl I only knew then as Miriam. She pointed to the rear of the store at the telephone booth. I looked, and all I could then see was a mass of fur. It appeared as if a bear was making a telephone call. I waited and waited where I stood. In time, I heard the door to the telephone booth open, and out stepped this girl in a fur coat. She was beautiful. I was immediately smitten with her. As we greeted, I noticed Gus, as we called Mel by nickname, already had the girl who was sitting at the counter in tow.

We left the drugstore and went to a place called Ma Downer's out in South Wellfleet. There wasn't any place else to go in those days, because they rolled the sidewalks up in the town of Wellfleet at seven p.m. Ma Downer's was just a shack, a small place where one could sit and have a cup of coffee or drink a beer. It wasn't a very exciting date for any of us; we just sat around talking and carved our initials on the wooden table. At least we were inside, away from the cold. This was Cape Cod nightlife in 1950. I found myself taken with Miriam, however, and found her to be more intelligent in conversation than me.

Sometime later, we left Ma Downer's and drove around Wellfleet for a while. I picked a spot and stopped the car. I kissed Miriam, and bells began to ring in my head. Something had happened to me like never before. No sooner had my head cleared and I was wanting an encore than Miriam said she had to go home. I thought at the time perhaps I had offended her, or that I wasn't a very good kisser. As I found out later, she also heard bells and wasn't sure what it meant. We dropped the girls off at Miriam's house, and during the drive back to Chatham, I told Gus, "I'm going to marry that girl." Gus, of course, told me I was crazy and didn't know what I was talking about.

One the next date I had with Miriam, she insisted that I had to meet her folks. I wasn't exactly thrilled at the idea. But she said she wouldn't go out with me unless I did. Arriving at the old lovely Cape Cod-style home of Miriam's parents on Cross Street, I got out of the car and was met at the door of the sun porch by Miriam. Upon entering, the first thing I noticed about the place was a shotgun hanging on the wall.

I wondered then if this was an indication of things to come.

Inside, when I entered, there they were sitting proud and stern: Ma and Pa Pentinen, Otto and Olga, true Finlanders who had immigrated to the United States many years before. From the way they talked with me, it was obvious they were interested in what was best for their daughter. They appeared concerned about this sailor their daughter had brought home. Olga was a devout Christian and a stalwart member of the Women's Christian Temperance Union. About all I had going for me was that I was the son of a Baptist minister, a fact that seemed to please Olga.

Ma and Pa Pentinen allowed Miriam and me to go out for a while that night and to continue dating through the long, cold winter. One night when Miriam and I were parked in the old Plymouth out at Nauset Beach, with the car's heater running, she asked me to marry her. Shaken by her question—it scared me—I blurted out a "No." She then said, "Very well then take me home." I was driving her home, thinking all the while, "I really do love this girl." It was, after all, still winter; she was beautiful; and I didn't want to lose her.

Thinking, during the trip to her home, about what she had asked me, I stopped the car upon arriving and looked at her and said, "OK." She looked at me and said, "OK, What?" I replied, "OK, I'll marry you." She thought for a moment and then said, "when?" I then told her to name a date, and she determined our marriage should take place on July 16 for some reason. I agreed. It was now March, and that would give us four months to make plans. Also, I would have to obtain permission from my commanding officer at Chatham lifeboat station, Alvin Newcomb.

As it turned out, we were to have a small family wedding at my home in Milton, Massachusetts. My father, the Reverend A. Bernard Webber, would officiate. Arrangements made, the day arrived. On July 16th, we were married. Dad performed our ceremony. It was strange to have my father officiate, and it was even somewhat more awkward for Miriam, as she knew the minister would now be her father-in-law. I think we both realized that he must have approved of the

July 16, 1950; the joyous newlyweds united in marriage at the Webber family home in East Milton, Massachusetts.

Miriam excited and happy as a new bride leaving the home of her inlaws the Rev A. Bernard and Annie Webber resplendent in her hand-tailored suit and purse she had made for her special day. Rose petals and rice thrown, Bernie and Miriam now off to their honeymoon.

marriage by performing our ceremony. To be sure, my dad, the minister, tied the knot, retied it, then tied it again. Baptist ministers have a thing about not leaving any stone unturned—they cover all ground, in such circumstances, no matter how long it takes.

Once married to Miriam, I also felt truly united with Cape Cod. At first, we took up residence in a little upstairs apartment located in a building next door to the curtain factory in Wellfleet. I got home from the lifeboat station once every ten days. The two days I would then have off were just not enough for two newly married young people. As a result, later on, we moved to Chatham and rented a place named Silver Heels on Sea View Street.

Living at Silver Heels was a rewarding experience. Not only was I able to sneak home more often, but Miriam and I became closer to the town and the people. While I was up at the Coast Guard station, she worked in the local First National Store, which helped out financially, since I didn't make much money.

We made good friends throughout the town. One such friendship was that of John and Jean Stello, who lived across the street. John was a Chatham fisherman and, with his boat, *Jeannie S*, was one of the Highliners—a term denoting a very successful boat whose waterline is high because it is literally weighed down with fish. The many nights Miriam and I spent at the Stellos' either just talking or playing cards were memorable for us and appreciated at the time. Through John and Jean we continued to meet many of their friends, which further developed our closeness to the people of Chatham.

Living at Silver Heels was a good period for Miriam and me. Then things happened at the Coast Guard station that changed our lives.

The Changing Chatham Town

Not long after Miriam and I moved to Chatham, we noticed an air of excitement seemed to be developing within the town. Events taking place out at the Coast Guard station and other things happening around town gave the appearance the town was gearing up for something.

First, a movie was being made in the town of Chatham, using local people and coastguardsmen. The movie was to be about Cap Cod, its people, and their relationship with the sea. However, the name of the movie was to become "Cape Cod Coast Guardsmen." Dave Ryder, a local fisherman, played the leading role. Several other local people had parts in the production. Some of the sequences in the movie called for the Coast Guard to assist the local fishermen in scenes where their vessel would be in distress. At the time, I would operate the Coast Guard motor lifeboat or amphibious Coast Guard vehicle called a DUKW. After getting all wet or dirty during the process, I would hear the director say, "cut," then I was asked to get out of the equipment while a clean good-looking fellow by the name of Mahlon Chase got aboard for the close-up shots. Mahlon was a boatswain's mate at Chatham also.

He was better looking than me and photogenic, which I was not.

The experience of being part of the movie production was very interesting, but it was even more interesting to observe how some of the local people reacted to their part in the movie. There were those who really got caught up in the show-business mood. They began to dress, act, and talk like Hollywood. The movie, to my knowledge, didn't amount to much in the end, and I heard no more about it after it was made in Chatham. However, a good time was had by those of us who took part in it.

First Class Boatswain's Mate Mahlon Chase standing aboard CG36500 at Chatham Fish Pier, 1952. (Photo from the Author's collection.)

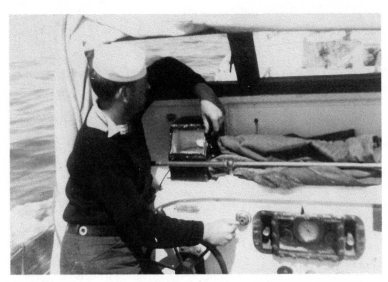

Bernie Webber aboard CG36383, 1950. (Photo from the Author's collection.)

At the Coast Guard station during this period, a lookout tower was in the process of being built. Located in front of the Chatham Lighthouse, the steel framework was already in place, and the house on top was under construction. The new lookout tower would replace the old watch room in the station below.

Planned, also, was the complete renovation of the old lighthouse keeper's quarters. That had been used as space for the lifeboat station crew for the past several years. A large addition to this building was to be built at the rear. The whole station was to be upgraded and modernized in order to provide better service to the community.

In addition to the movie being made and the construction going on at the lifeboat station, other things were taking place. For instance, more vessels started fishing out of Chatham. Many new boats came from Provincetown and other places to work out of Chatham. For those of us in the Coast Guard, our contract and association with the fishermen seemed to increase.

Chatham lifeboat station was always a busy place, but it was even busier now. Many of the fishing boats were old, the engines worn out, and the owners too poor to build a new boat or furnish what they had with a new engine. There were other fishermen who were quite wealthy as a result of the combination of luck and good business practices.

We in the Coast Guard became close to the poor fishermen because we came in contact with them more. We would tow their boats in frequently. There were many times a fisherman down on his luck would come to the Coast Guard station and ask for gasoline for his boat so that he could go out and fish that day. Although we knew we could be court-martialed for doing so, we would give them the gas they needed. Not one ever failed to pay the government back.

The Chatham fishermen and *their* Coast Guards formed a close bond. We knew their problems; they knew ours. We all helped each other. Gathering around the old wood stove at the Chatham Fish Pier during cold, stormy winter nights, we often maintained vigil together, watching the boats straining on their moorings in the harbor, aware we were all there to help one another when the need arose.

Almost daily, the motor lifeboat CG36500 could be seen operating in the area. She was either underway to one of the lightships, transporting personnel and supplies, or she could be seen with a disabled fishing boat in tow. Perhaps you would see her working down on Chatham Bar with the Chatham harbormaster Harold Claflin onboard, along with the Coast Guard crew, moving the buoys around to conform with the latest change in the channel. CG36500 was a familiar sight indeed.

Scalloper Muriel & Russell
Ashore and Breaking Up

The new lookout tower at Chatham lifeboat station was no sooner completed during the winter of 1950 than an observant watchman at the crack of dawn noticed strange activity over on North Beach. The weather was bad. A storm was in progress, with strong winds blowing out of the east. The seas were running high on the beach.

Ed Massey, the station cook, had come on watch at 0400. As dawn cracked, he looked through his binoculars, scanning along the beach. Suddenly he saw something amid the blackness of the ocean and the whiteness of seas cresting and breaking upon the beach. As he watched, a shape began to form. The light of day grew stronger, and he recognized the shape as that of a vessel. Soon he observed yellow figures upon its decks, appearing to be climbing the rigging. He knew a vessel was in trouble and left the tower to alert Frank Masachi, who was in charge of the station at that time.

We had heard that the fishing vessel *Muriel & Russell* was overdue at New Bedford from a trip off of Georges

Bank. She had not been heard from, but there was no cause for alarm as it was assumed her progress had been slowed by the storm. The Coast Guard stations had been alerted to just keep a watch out for her.

My room was across from Frank's. I heard the clomp of Massey's feet as he came up the stairs and into Frank's room. Ed stammered a bit when excited. I heard him trying to explain what he had seen to Frank. Upon hearing about yellow men running around, Frank bolted up, asking Massey if he had gone crazy. Ed finally was able to explain to Frank what he had seen. Frank went down to the office, picked up his binoculars, and opened the front door to look toward North Beach. Sure enough, Frank then knew there was a vessel, and it appeared to have hit the beach and was rolling around in the surf.

Frank gathered Stan Dauphinais and me as his crew. We manned the station's old World War II DUKW and drove across Old Harbor to the other side, landing on North Beach. Sure enough, a large fishing vessel was ashore. Its crew was sliding down over the bow as the vessel rolled in the surf. Landing in the water beneath, they scrambled up on to the beach, where we helped them. The entire eleven-man crew got off safely.

The tide was receding fast. Dauphinais and I clambered up over the vessel's bow to get aboard and see if we could save any of the expensive equipment on board. No sooner had we reached the pilothouse than we heard a crack and looked back to see the vessel's deck breaking open. We scrambled and got off quick.

We hit the beach and gathered the fishing vessel's crew in the DUKW. The *Muriel & Russell* was completely destroyed by the breaking surf. Nothing remained to indicate she had even been there. The loss of the vessel was sad. However, as we found out, Captain Strange and his crew had been bailing for two days, trying to keep the old boat afloat. Its seams had opened from the heavy seas of the storm. Their radio was not working, so they were unable to alert anyone. They just bailed and headed for the nearest land. Fortunately, they made it, and eleven men lived to fish again.

Transfers
A New Broom and a New Station

Shortly after the incident with the fishing vessel *Muriel
& Russell,* our well-liked and respected commanding
officer, Alvin E. Newcomb, was transferred from
Chatham lifeboat station to the Coast Guard base at
Woods Hole and served as executive officer for that
facility. For those of us at Chatham who had grown up
and developed as lifeboat men, he was greatly missed.

A young, newly promoted warrant officer by the
name of Daniel W. Cluff was assigned to the station
in Alvin Newcomb's place as the new officer in charge.
Mr. Cluff came from Chincoteague, Virginia, and spoke
with a dialect common to that part of the country.
From the moment of Daniel Cluff's arrival to take
charge, he represented a "new broom" to us that was to
sweep clean all that had been traditional at the station
under Newcomb's command.

Mr. Cluff inherited a station that was by now
almost completely rebuilt and modernized. The newly
built lookout tower even had a radar installation in it
to aid the unit's operations. Most of all, Cluff inherited
a crew of men well trained and experienced under the
kind hand of his predecessor. From the beginning,

there was a language barrier between Cluff and his crew of lifeboat men. Through no fault of his, he didn't speak our language, and we certainly didn't speak his. As a result, most of us just went along without question, nodding our heads and agreeing with whatever he said. Such was not the case with the old hard-nosed Chief Boatswain's Mate Frank Masachi. It was obvious that Frank resented Daniel Cluff. Frank didn't like the way Cluff operated the station or the privileges he appeared to take for himself. Cluff went home early every night to the house he was renting in Chatham; he didn't get involved in the boat work at the station; and he spent most of his time in developing personal relations in the area. For Frank, who had long worked under Newcomb, the manner in which Cluff operated the lifeboat station went against his grain. From the beginning between Daniel Cluff and Frank Masachi, it was the civil war all over again—the North against the South. It wasn't long before Frank requested a transfer and left Chatham to serve on a Coast Guard rescue vessel CG83388 as the officer in charge, operating out of Woods Hole.

Replacing Frank Masachi at the station was Chief Boatswain's Mate Donald Bangs. Donald was an experienced, very knowledgeable fellow who was easygoing and loved to converse. Cluff and Bangs got along very well together, which relieved tension for the rest of us.

As time went on, Chief Bangs pretty well ran the station operations and dealt with the men. Bos'n Cluff was preoccupied with the contractors putting the final touches on the newly rebuilt facility.

When the contractors had finished their work, the whole inside of the station had been gutted and rebuilt into modern quarters. A large addition built onto the rear of the station housed a mess hall and galley, which would make any renowned chef proud. Upstairs was a dormitory. The station crew now had a poolroom in the basement. Everything at the place was new. Furniture, beds, you name it, Chatham lifeboat station now had it. It was a showplace for the Coast Guard.

Some of us sensed that all these changes that had taken place were for some special reason. Call it psychic, if you will, but I, for one, thought about the time I had now spent at Chatham, the events that I had participated in, and the relations I had developed with fishermen and local townspeople. For me, it all seemed to have a purpose. I had a total familiarity with the town and the surrounding waters. I knew every inch of the territory and understood the elements.

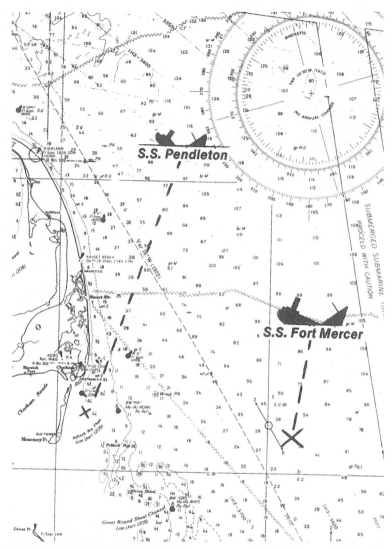

This is a reproduction of the Coast and Geodetic Survey Chart No.
1107. The wrecks of the Pendleton and Fort Mercer are drawn in
at the approximate locations where they broke up and drifted in the
storm. The stern of the Pendleton grounded about a mile off Monomoy
Island. The bow was towed to Providence, Rhode Island, and cut up
for scrap. The stern of the Fort Mercer was salvaged, and a new bow
added. She was renamed the San Jacinto, and a few years later, she
again broke in half in a storm. Afterward, she was cut up for scrap.

Chatham's Finest Hours
The Day a Community Worked Together

18 February 1952

This was to be a particular day that I believe God planned and directed especially for the town of Chatham. It would become a day in which many were touched in one way or the other by the events that took place. A community would be challenged in many varied ways. The response to the challenges became an example of human good.

New England, and in particular the outer coast of Cape Cod, was in the midst of a fierce storm. A nor'easter was blowing, with winds seventy miles per hour or more and wind-driven snow that was of blizzard proportions. Extremely heavy seas were running offshore forty to sixty feet in height.

The town of Chatham was receiving the brunt of this storm. The people of this town were all too familiar with what could happen on land or sea during gales such as this. However, no one could have imagined the events that would occur in Chatham this day.

During the morning, the local people were busy digging out of the snow that blanketed Chatham. Efforts were made to concentrate on keeping the lifelines of needed services open. Fishermen stood by down at the Chatham Fish Pier around the old wood stove. Peering out the windows, they intently watched their boats on moorings, with lines taut, bouncing up and down in the waves, nearly breaking under the strain. They stood and waited as their boats pitched up and down and swayed back and forth, dancing to waves that Old Harbor in Chatham had rarely seen before. Each fisherman was preoccupied with his own thoughts—concerned about the possibility that his boat might break loose and be destroyed, which would mean the end of his livelihood.

• • •

By midmorning, Chatham lifeboat station received word about a ship in distress. The tanker SS *Fort Mercer* had broken in half some forty miles out to sea from Chatham. The two ship sections were drifting helplessly in the raging seas with men aboard in peril and requiring assistance. Then, the telephone at the station continued to ring with calls from local fishermen, requesting the Coast Guard aid them as their boats were breaking away from moorings in the harbor.

All of a sudden, Chatham lifeboat station was becoming very busy, and the pace would continue to pick up through the remainder of the day. Every resource of the station would become drained. Bos'n Cluff received orders to dispatch a motor lifeboat out to the aid of the tanker *Fort Mercer*. When I heard about it, I couldn't believe my ears. I thought, "My God, do they really think a lifeboat and its crew could actually make it that far out to sea in this storm and find the broken ship amid the blinding snow and a raging sea with only a compass to guide them? If the crew of the lifeboat didn't freeze to death first, how would they be able to get the men off the storm-tossed sections of the broken tanker?"

Regardless of my thought about the matter, I soon heard Bos'n Cluff order Chief Donald Bangs to select a crew, then proceed down to Stage Harbor and man the motor lifeboat CG36383; further, to proceed out to the position of the *Fort Mercer*. Cluff, then turning to me, ordered that I take a crew and go down to Old Harbor to help the local fishermen. I was to use the motor lifeboat CG36500 and go out into the harbor and attempt to pull boats off the beach where they had gone after breaking their moorings.

Chief Bangs chose for his crew Engineman First Class Emory H. Haynes, Boatswain's Mate Third Class (Provisional) Antonia F. Ballerini, and Seaman Richard J. Ciccone. As these men left the station, I felt as if I was watching them go off to certain death. Close to them all, I wondered if I would ever see them again.

Shortly after Bangs left, my crew and I departed for the local fish pier and manned the motor lifeboat CG36500. We were to spend the next few hours with local fisherman, helping them retrieve their boats and return them to moorings in Old Harbor.

By midafternoon, we had finished our task. We were very cold and tired from the biting snow and winds that had cut into us the past several hours. I rejoiced that we would soon be able to go back to the station and its warmth and comfort. We secured the CG36500 on its mooring and rowed ashore in our dory. I thought about Chief Bangs and his crew—how cold and miserable they must be by now.

These thoughts were soon put aside. When we landed on the beach in the dory, Bos'n Cluff met us. He said another ship by the name of SS *Pendleton*, a T2 tanker, had also broken in half offshore and was expected to move in close somewhere along North Beach between Orleans and Chatham. Cluff ordered me with my crew to take the Dodge Power Wagon truck and head for the town of Orleans. Once there, we were to meet up with Roy Piggott, George Rongner, and the Nauset lifeboat station crew in the DUKW. Together, we were to proceed out to Nauset Beach and attempt to locate the stricken vessel and render aid should it come ashore.

The trip from Chatham to Orleans in the truck was made hazardous by the high winds, icy roads, and drifts of snow. Fortunately, the four-wheeled vehicle plowed on through. We were comforted and warmed by the truck's heater, a luxury Donald Bangs and his crew certainly didn't have.

When we arrived at Orleans, Piggott and his crew were waiting. Together, we headed out to Nauset Beach. Arriving at the top of the hill near Mayo's duck farm, we stopped our vehicles. The panoramic view from this point allowed us scan miles of shoreline. Through the snow, we could see great waves breaking upon the

This is how the tanker Pendleton *was before the breakup in the storm 18 February 1952. (Photo from the Author's collection.)*

beach and running high up on the land. As we peered through eyes stinging from the biting wind and flakes of snow, an object darker than the ocean was seen out beyond the crashing waves.

A brief shift in the weather showed us a ship, black and sinister, galloping along up and down huge waves, frothing each time it rose or settled back into the sea. We knew it had to be the stern of the tanker *Pendleton* that Bos'n Cluff had indicated. Pushed by wind and seas, the hulk was rapidly heading south toward Chatham.

We got back in our truck, turned it around, and with the Nauset crew in the DUKW, raced toward Chatham over the icy roads. As we didn't have any means of communicating with the Chatham station, we had to go in person to spread the alarm.

Arriving back at the station around 1730 (5:30 p.m.), it was near darkness. On the station's radar, two objects were seen. One appeared offshore several miles and headed toward Pollock Rip Lightship. It was believed to be the bow of the tanker *Pendleton* because the other object had been also visually seen and was believed to be the stern section of the *Pendleton* close off the coastline. In fact, local people had observed the hulk and heard the blowing of its whistle as it wallowed along.

Bos'n Cluff was now under great pressure. He knew he had to do something. There were certainly men aboard the sections, and they needed help. Chief Bangs and his crew reached the bow section of the *Pendleton* and found no life on board. He was then diverted to the stern section. However, a ship close by the bow section observed a man, and Bangs was then ordered to return to it. Bos'n Cluff made up his mind.

I sensed Cluff's course of action. My suspicion was confirmed when I heard him say, "Webber, pick yourself a crew. Y'all got to take the 36500 out over the bar and assist that thar ship, ya-heah?" I heard, all right, it took a moment for me to digest his words. A sinking feeling came over me. I thought about many things before answering him.

My wife was home at Silver Heels, sick in bed. I hadn't spoken with her for two days. I knew that taking a lifeboat out over Chatham Bar would be risky business, with little chance of success. Yes, I wondered why he had chosen me when there were others that could be considered for the mission. "Yes Sir, Mr. Cluff, I'll get ready." It was logical for me to make the attempt. After all, I knew the waters and the territory better than anyone else. Somehow, I also knew in the back of my mind that GC36500 had been a special attraction for me since 1946 when I first saw her. Perhaps this journey was to be the reason.

I knew whom I wanted to take with me as my crew. However, as I looked around the station, I couldn't find them. Only three men were standing by, none of whom I considered as likely candidates for such a perilous voyage. Time was of the essence. The three men looked at me and almost in unison said, "Bernie, we'll go with you if you want." I accepted their offer. It was to be the best decision I ever made. Engineman Andrew J. Fitzgerald, Seaman Richard P. Livesey, and Seaman Irving Maske were to be my crew. Maske especially didn't have to volunteer. He wasn't even assigned to Chatham station. He just happened to be awaiting transportation back out to his assigned duties at Stonehorse Lightship.

Together, we departed the lifeboat station and drove down to the Chatham Fish Pier. Upon arriving, we were getting the dory ready to row out to the GC36500 mooring when a voice above us up on the pier yelled out, "You guys better get lost before you get too far out." I recognized fisherman John Stello, my neighbor who lived across the street from Silver Heels. I yelled back to him and said, "Call Miriam and let her know what's going on." I knew what John meant and respected his knowledge and experience. It made me uneasy, knowing that John was expressing doubts that we would even make it over the bar.

At 1755 (5:55 p.m.), we departed the Chatham Fish Pier in the motor lifeboat CG36500, the ninety-horsepower gas engine sputtering along, not yet warmed up. As we headed out Old Harbor, darkness was upon us, lights ashore were dimmed through flurries of snow. As we made a turn in the channel,

An artist's rendition of rescuers setting out on the 36500.

Chatham Lighthouse came into view, the powerful light sweeping over us each time the lens rotated. We could see the dim lights glowing from the main building. I wondered what was going on inside, hoping for a call on our radio that would direct us to return. I called the station just in case. Word came back: "Proceed as directed." I don't know why but, for some reason, we all began to sing songs like "Rock of Ages" and "Harbor Lights." Unexplained, peculiar for young men who normally never think about or know the words to such songs.

We were nearing the bar. Just below the bluff of Morris Island, I could hear the roar of the ocean breaking on the Chatham bars ahead of us. We were already cold; our clothing was not waterproof so we were wet clear through. The buckle-type rubber overshoes we wore provided no warmth for already-cold feet. Looking at the men around me, I knew they were depending upon my judgment. I could turn around and go back, saying the bar was too rough for us to make it over. Nobody would have criticized us. After all, I had heard what John Stello had said.

Moving the lifeboat CG36500 closer to Chatham Bar, I called the lifeboat station again, with one last hope that they would direct us to return. Instead, we were informed that it was imperative that we proceed out over the bar and head for sea.

At that point, a shiver went through me. Questions came to my mind. Where were we to go? With only a magnetic compass to navigate by, no radar to assist us in locating a broken ship in the blackness of a night full of sleet, snow, and raging seas, how could we possibly do it?

If we were fortunate in find the *Pendleton*, would there be any survivors on board? If so, how could we possibly get them off the wreck under stormy conditions? If I were to head out over the bar, would I be jeopardizing the four lives onboard CG36500 in a vain attempt? Never faced with a situation where the matter of life or death rested totally on my decisions, I was overwhelmed with the responsibility now resting on my conscience. Did I know what I was doing? Was I capable of using good judgment? I thought once again about my wife at home sick in bed. All these things came to mind.

I reasoned that I was a Coast Guard first class boatswain's mate. My job was the sea and to save those in peril upon it. I thought also about all those I had grown up with in the Coast Guard: Frank Masachi, Alvin Newcomb, Alfred Volton, Leo Gracie, and many others, too numerous to mention, who had shown me the way. I then knew what, traditionally, I had to do.

Without further thought, I told my crew to hang on, then revved up the lifeboat's engine and headed into the blackness of Chatham Bar. Fortunately, I really couldn't see the conditions ahead. I wasn't aware of what was about to happen, otherwise I might have turned around right there and then and headed back in.

The first sea we encountered smashed into CG36500, tossing it up in the air and landing it far down between the waves on its side. No sooner had we recovered than another mountainous wave struck. The little lifeboat shuddered under the impact of tons of water. The glass in the windshield in front of me shattered, and a torrent of water came through the opening, knocking me down. The compass was ripped from its mount. I held on to the steering wheel for life, trying to head the boat back into the seas before we broached. It took all the strength I could muster.

No thought was given now of turning the lifeboat around. Any attempt to do so surely would have cap-sized us. Another great wave hit and laid the lifeboat far over on its side. The engine stopped. Evidently, the severe thrashing we were subjected to and the acute angle placed on the little vessel caused the engine to lose its prime of gasoline. Andrew Fitzgerald would crawl into the engine compartment each time it happened and restart the motor. It was no easy task for Andrew to get into the compartment of the wildly tossing boat. He suffered many bruises and burns during his efforts. Had Andrew Fitzgerald not made the extreme effort to keep our little ninety-horsepower motor operating, we all would have perished.

Somehow, we kept going. Eventually the seas changed a bit. They took on greater height but were spaced further apart. This indicated to me we were in deeper water, a sign that we must have cleared the Chatham Bar and now were on the outside. I kept the lifeboat headed into the mountains ahead. Our progress was awkward. It was a long, slow climb to the top of the waves. Once there, we would fall ahead and race down the other side to the point where our forward motion was so fast I would have to reverse the lifeboat in order to slow it down. Otherwise, it would bury itself.

I didn't know where we were or how far we had come. All I knew was that as long as I headed into the waves, we would be moving in a direction toward Pollack Rip Lightship and the open ocean. I hoped to catch a glimpse of the lightship and make our way over to her, and at least find some comfort in knowing where we were. By now, we all were worn out from the wet and cold, and tense from the experience. There seemed to be no let up in the weather; in fact it appeared to be worsening, if that was possible. All we could do was ride it out.

So it went in the blackness of night in the cutting wind with snow biting our faces. Andy, Richard, and Irving crowded together to one side of the coxswain flat with their lifejackets on, hanging on to the pipe rail for support, giving me all the room they could so I would be able to steer and maneuver the boat. I opted not to wear a lifejacket in order to have more freedom with my arms to steer the boat. I wondered if they were warmer than I, since they had lifejackets on.

We continued along in CG36500 for some time, battling the sea. I was becoming concerned that perhaps we had gone too far and missed Pollock Lightship. I had lost track of time. I called on our radio to the lightship and to Chatham station, but there was no reply. We seemed to be all alone. I began to think about the fact that it would be daylight in ten or twelve hours. The question came to mind of whether we could last that long.

Suddenly, as I peered out through the opening in the lifeboat's windshield, a strange feeling came over me. It appeared that a blackness much darker than I had been peering into existed ahead of us. I was so uncomfortable with this feeling that I slowed CG36500 down, almost to a stop. Then I asked one of the crew to go forward on the lifeboat and turn on the little search-light mounted on the forward cabin.

The form of a man went forward, crawling along, hanging on to the grab rails. A moment later, the light came on. In an instant in the glow of the searchlight, I saw a man tossed up in the air by a wave that struck the boat. He appeared carried away by it. Then a thump behind where I was steering announced the man was carried back on board.

Moving ahead slowly and peering into the searchlight's path, suddenly I saw what appeared to be a tunnel's entrance—and we were headed into it. This tunnel was a mass of broken, twisted steel. It would rise up high in front of us, then settle back down in a frothing mass of foam. Each time it rose up out of the ocean, it appeared like a waterfall. Sounds came from it, a clanging and banging of loose steel beams and plates. Each time it settled back down, it groaned as if in pain. I knew we had found the *Pendleton.*

Very slowly and at a distance, I maneuvered the CG36500 around the hulk, keeping it within reach of the searchlight's beam. Once away from the mass of brokenness and heading down the port side of the ship, it was apparent that no lights were to be seen and no sign of life. High up on her decks, the rails were twisted and broken. Other destruction was obvious. I then felt that I had made a poor decision in bringing these men out here to suffer as they already had. Evidently, everyone on board the *Pendleton* had already perished. This was a useless trip that endangered the lives of my own crew.

I continued to maneuver the CG36500 down along the ship's port side. Reaching a position off the stern, I looked up and could make out the name *Pendleton* dimly in the glow from our searchlight. Rounding the stern, suddenly there were lights high up on the ship's deck. I couldn't believe my eyes. This meant that there was power on board the hulk, therefore there must be life on board. Sure enough, there was a figure waving his arms. He looked very tiny, way up there on the deck. Then he disappeared. I wondered why until I saw him

Tony Falcone's painting Rescue of the Pendleton *by the 36500. See page 172 for more information.*

return with a procession of people that nearly filled the starboard side of the ship, all along the rails. I was stunned by the spectacle. I positioned the boat closer to the hulk to get a better look. Men high above us waved their arms and we could hear voices yelling but were unable to distinguish what they were saying. At the moment, their position looked inviting to me. They looked safer up on the stern of the ruined *Pendleton* than I felt at the moment down in the CG36500. I thought about how we could get up there.

The men on the *Pendleton* thought differently. Before I knew it, they had thrown a Jacob's ladder over the side, fastened from the deck level above. Some of them started down it. I thought, good Lord, they are coming over the side and want us to pick them off the ladder! The man now at the bottom of the ladder was dunked each time the ship rolled over in the sea. One moment he would be under water, the next he would rise up high in the air. I moved CG36500 in close to the hull of the *Pendleton*, timing my maneuver so as to be alongside at the right moment to let a man jump for our boat. My crew were now forward on CG36500, hanging on for dear life, waiting to catch the *Pendleton* crewmen as they came aboard.

I made several passes with the CG36500, and each time, a man jumped for the lifeboat. Landing hard on the forward deck, he would be grabbed by my crew and stuffed in the forward cabin. Other *Pendleton* crewmen waiting on the ladder would be swung out in the air one moment as the ship laid over, only to be slammed up against the hull as the ship rolled the other way. I wondered how they could possibly hang on, but they did, patiently waiting our return alongside.

When we had fifteen or twenty of the crewmen aboard the lifeboat. I realized it was getting crowded, heavy in the water and harder for me to maneuver. I didn't think we could take any more men aboard the lifeboat. The choice was not mine, however, as the remaining *Pendleton* crewmen kept coming over the side and down the ladder. They were frantic now to get off the broken hulk. When we got the CG36500 close, they would jump off the ladder too soon. Five or so missed and landed in the water. Fortunately my alert crew exposed themselves and hung out far over the side of the lifeboat and grabbed the men in the water. Somehow, with superhuman strength, they brought the survivors on board.

There were several men left aboard the *Pendleton*, and I contemplated leaving them there as the CG36500 was riding very heavy in the water. I didn't know how we could go anywhere with the load I already had on board. I just couldn't leave them, though, so I decided to go for broke. Either we would all live or we would all die. Continuing the process, we eventually had them all aboard except one. He was hanging at the bottom of the Jacob's ladder, first thrown out in the air, then slapped up against the side of the ship. Each time he hit, I thought I could hear him groan. This was a very big man—at least three hundred pounds. He was nearly naked and presented a cumbersome sight. I learned later he was George (Tiny) Myers and that he had been an inspiration for the other *Pendleton* crewmen and had helped them off the stricken ship before thinking of himself.

In the beam from the lifeboat's searchlight, I watched Tiny hanging on at the bottom of the ladder. I headed the lifeboat toward him in an attempt to pick him off. The ocean seemed rougher and the wind more forceful, and the CG36500 handled very poorly. It was sluggish to steer and very heavy with our human load. *Pendleton* survivors were everywhere onboard the CG36500. The forward compartment was stuffed full of men, as was the engine compartment. Men were crammed around my steering station and filled the after space onboard the little lifeboat.

We were closer to Tiny when he suddenly jumped for us, but it was too soon. He was swallowed up in the sea, and we lost sight of him. I steered the lifeboat away from the side of the *Pendleton* and came around in a circle. One of my crewmen was shining our forward searchlight all around the waters surrounding the ship. Then we saw him. Tiny was now down under the very stern of the *Pendleton,* hanging on to the side of a propeller blade. These blades were about eleven feet long. There were three of them, and they were sticking mostly out of the water due to the angle of the ship.

Once again, I headed the CG36500 toward Tiny. It was going to be very difficult to retrieve him from his position. It meant I would have to stick the bow of the lifeboat directly toward him and see if we could get close enough to grab ahold of him. I eased ahead with the lifeboat. Suddenly I felt our stern rise up and knew a big sea was coming from behind. The seas began to push us ahead at a rapid pace toward Tiny. I reversed the lifeboat's engine in hopes of backing away, all the time watching Tiny's face, looking into his eyes, seeing the fright on his face. It was too late. The lifeboat was pushed ahead, out of control and too sluggish to respond to any effort I made to steer clear. I was backing the lifeboat full speed when we hit the *Pendleton*, smashing also into Tiny Myers.

The lifeboat was washed out from the derelict when another big sea hit us. In the glow from our searchlight I saw the *Pendleton* rise up and roll over, the deck lights went out, and the hulk disappeared from view. Except for our searchlight on the lifeboat there was darkness all around us. I told the men forward to shut off. I felt sick to my stomach over the loss of Tiny.

We were now alone in the blackness of storm-tossed seas somewhere off Chatham. Motor lifeboat CG36500 held thirty-two survivors from the tanker SS *Pendleton* and four Coast Guard crewmen. Thirty-six men on a thirty-six-foot Coast Guard motor lifeboat. I didn't know where we were, and we didn't have a compass. All I knew was that if I headed into the seas, the open ocean lay ahead all the way to Europe. If we went with the seas, putting them astern, land lay somewhere up ahead.

I called the Chatham lifeboat station on the CG36500's radio. They answered right away, which surprised me. Earlier, we had lost radio communications. I then informed the station about our situation—

that we had onboard thirty-two survivors from the tanker *Pendleton* and all other details regarding our condition. There was a pause before the station acknowledged my transmission. I think mostly because it was hard for them to believe we had actually rescued so many men and had them aboard the little lifeboat.

Then it started. The airwaves were now full of questions directed at me. Chatham station wanted to know many more details. A large Coast Guard cutter offshore called and tried to take over the situation by directing that we proceed out to sea and bring the survivors to them. I could hear the arguments going on between units as to what we should do, and in typical government-service fashion, who was responsible for what and who outranked whom.

I had heard all I wanted to hear. Knowing that none of them could do a thing to help our situation, I shut off the radio in the CG36500. By then I was too tired, cold, and just plain worn out to have any part of it. I knew the fate of the *Pendleton* survivors, the Coast Guard crewmen, and, yes, that of CG36500, rested squarely on my shoulders. There was no way we could head out to sea and get the men of the *Pendleton* safely aboard a Coast Guard cutter smaller than the tanker we had taken them from. Many survivors were in a state of shock or otherwise hurt. All suffered from exposure. I was aware that it was next to impossible that I could find my way to Chatham. After weighing all the circumstances, I made my decision.

I knew we were somewhere off Chatham or Monomoy Island; perhaps even to the south of

Monomoy. In any case, I knew if I put the ocean waves behind the little lifeboat and just let them push us along, land lay somewhere up ahead. Even if we missed the point of Monomoy, we would enter Nantucket Sound, which was surrounded with land and that offered hope for our survival.

The word about my plan was passed to all those aboard the motor lifeboat CG36500. I told those around me that I was heading shoreward. Further, if and when they felt the boat hit the shore somewhere, to just clamber off the lifeboat out over the bow. I would keep the lifeboat in gear and hold her onto any beach as long as I could to enable them to get free. After I explained the whole situation to them, one of the *Pendleton* survivors yelled out, "We're with you, Coxswain"; then, as if in agreement, a cheer went up around me. I felt relieved that I had their approval of what I was about to do.

From then on, we moved along slowly in the CG36500, allowing the winds and waves to just push us. The men aboard were silent. The only sounds to be heard were the wind whistling around, the sea crashing aboard, and the low roar of the lifeboat's engine. Peering ahead into blackness, I realized I felt warmer now, evidently warmed by the many bodies standing around close to my steering station, pressing hard up against me each time the boat lurched. I thought about this human cargo onboard and what was to be of all thirty-six of us. I had second thoughts about where I was heading with these men.

Time dragged on with no sight of anything to give

us a clue as to where we were. I took notice, though, that the sea around us was different now. The waves were not as deep and far apart as they had been. They were more confused. This was an indication that the lifeboat was now in shallower waters. I knew then our situation could become even more dangerous as we were getting closer to shore. It was necessary, though, if I were to beach the lifeboat as planned.

Suddenly, I thought I saw something. Staring intently through the broken opening of the lifeboat's windshield, I saw it again. I thought at first my eyes were playing tricks on me. The spitting snow, burning salt spray, and small slivers of glass around my face and eyes led me to believe at first I was seeing an illusion. But there it was again, even clearer now. Yes, I was sure it was a red flashing light. It flashed again and again. I didn't know where it was coming from. It would at one time seem to flash high up in the air, another time it would appear down low on the waters ahead. All I could think of was that it was one of the Chatham RCA radio station towers that had aircraft-warning lights that flashed red up at the top of them.

The flashing red light offered comfort to me. It gave me something to head for although I was concerned that if it were the Chatham radio towers it would mean that if I beached the lifeboat, we would probably land on the isolated area of North Beach—not the best place for men in our situation. It wasn't long before I would not have to concern myself any further. The little red flashing light was soon close at hand. I yelled to men at the front of the lifeboat to turn on our searchlight.

When it came on, I was stunned. Directly ahead in the beam of our searchlight was a buoy, its light on top blinking red. I couldn't believe my eyes. I was elated, for immediately I recognized it. It was the buoy on the inside of Chatham Bar, at the turn marking the entrance up into Old Harbor. We were safe now. We were near home. Smooth waters lay ahead. All we needed to do was navigate the twists and turns of the harbor up to Aunt Lydia's Cove and the Chatham Fish Pier.

I called the Chatham lifeboat station from the lifeboat's radio and told them our position. An excited voice on the other end answered, indicating disbelief and shock that we were actually in Old Harbor. Almost immediately over the radio I began to receive instructions telling me to turn the lifeboat first one way then another. I realized that the person in the Chatham lookout tower was probably trying to pick us up on the radar and would try to be of help in guiding us up the harbor. However, the directions I received were of no use to me. I was very familiar with Old Harbor and had been up and down it many, many times. I knew where the shoal spots were and when the turns had to be made. I was in no mood to listen to the chatter on the radio. Too tired to be gracious under the circumstance, I called the lookout tower and said we would need assistance with the survivors when we reached the fish pier. Then I turned off our radio onboard the CG36500.

The lights of Chatham Fish Pier showed up ahead. I could hear the survivors around me. Some were talking excitedly; they knew they would now survive. Others were thanking God out loud. Yet, I could hear others sobbing. I wondered what it was like for those men stuffed into the little lifeboat's forward compartment. By now, they surely realized the sea was calm and we were safe, but they remained inside.

When we got close to the fish pier, I looked up and was overwhelmed by the crowd standing there—men, women, and even children of Chatham had turned out on this stormy night to greet and aid the survivors from SS *Pendleton.*

Someone grabbed our lines and tied our little lifeboat to the pier. Eager hands reached out and assisted the *Pendleton* survivors ashore, whisking them away to

The rescue boat CG36500 returned to the Chatham Fish Pier with thirty-two survivors from the tanker Pendleton *after the rescue at sea. Engineman Third Class Andrew Fitzgerald was on the bow ready to handle the tie-up at the pier. The other three men were* Pendleton *survivors. (Photo by Richard C. Kelsey, Chatham, Massachusetts. www.capecodphotos.com)*

The lifeboat was secured to the pier, and the survivors lined up along the side of the boat and climbed ashore for transportation to the Coast Guard station. (Photo by Richard C. Kelsey, Chatham, Massachusetts. www.capecodphotos.com)

warmth, food, and the care they so badly needed. I was drained; however, a warm glow came over me. I felt warm and comforted in knowing we all had reached the safety of shore.

I stood at the stern of this little lifeboat, her name only CG36500, and realized she had carried us out into the unknown on a mission of mercy. We had come from I didn't know where, to the safety of Chatham Harbor, crossing the bar. I began to tremble and sob. With my crewman Irving Maske beside me, I unashamedly cried in the near solitude and gave thanks to God for guiding us through the unknown.

After that, I didn't remember leaving the CG36500 or the trip over the road up to Chatham lifeboat station. When I came back to reality, I was sitting on my bunk upstairs at Chatham lifeboat station, bending over, taking off my overshoes. Chief Bill Woodman was talking to me. Feeling better, I wanted a cup of coffee and something to eat. I went downstairs to the galley. As I passed through the mess hall, I couldn't believe the commotion going on there. *Pendleton* survivors were sitting, standing, and lying around the room everywhere. Some were being attended to by Dr. Carroll Keene, Reverend Steve Smith, Ben Goodspeed, and others, receiving medical or spiritual attention as needed. Others were being measured up for clothing by Ben Shufro, manager of Puritan Clothing Store. Leroy Anderson and his fellow Red Cross workers were on hand to render aid.

I entered the galley. Bos'n Cluff was there, as was Richard Livesey, Andrew Fitzgerald, and Irving Maske. Mr. Cluff congratulated me and voiced his opinion that he didn't think he would see any of us alive again. Photographers were there, snapping pictures and asking questions. All I wanted was a cup of coffee and a good Cushman's doughnut. There was talk of heroes, rewards, and outstanding coastguardsmen. None of us at the time comprehended what the talk was all about. We were too exhausted and worn out from our experience. All we wanted to do was to go to bed. I went upstairs to bed and left all the noisy din behind. As I lay in my warm and comfortable bed, my thoughts and prayers were turned to those who this night remained at sea.

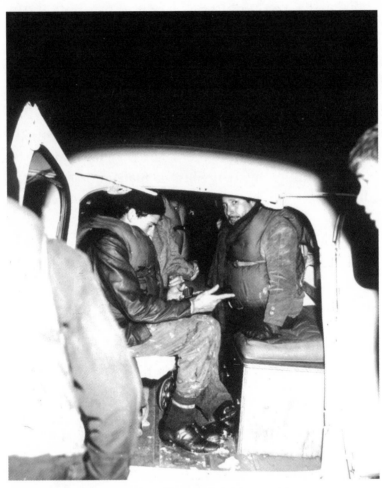

The Pendleton *survivors were loaded aboard trucks, station wagons, and cars for the short journey to the station. (Photo by Richard C. Kelsey, Chatham, Massachusetts. www.capecodphotos.com)*

Seaman Irving Maske (foreground) and Boatswain's Mate First Class Bernard Webber in the coxswain's flat aboard the CG36500 following the dramatic rescue of the thirty-two men off the stern of the Pendleton *on 18 February 1952. (Photo by Richard C. Kelsey, Chatham, Massachusetts. www.capecodphotos.com)*

Two survivors of the Pendleton *are interviewed by Ed Semprini of WOCB radio in South Yarmouth for broadcast all over the country. (Photo by Richard C. Kelsey, Chatham, Massachusetts. www.capecod-photos.com)*

The Gold Medal crew relaxed at the station with coffee and dough-nuts after a wild night at sea. Left to right: Boatswain's Mate First Class Bernard Webber, Engineman Third Class Andrew Fitzgerald, Seaman Richard Livesey, and Seaman Irving Maske. (Photo by Richard C. Kelsey, Chatham, Massachusetts. www.capecodphotos.com)

The bow of the Pendleton.
(Photo courtesy of the US Coast Guard, Washington, DC)

The Aftermath of the *Pendleton*

The next morning, staring at the ceiling above my bunk at the Chatham lifeboat station, I wondered if I had dreamed of being at sea in a storm or if I had actually taken part in the rescue of thirty-two men. Looking around the room, still half asleep, I noticed money lying on the floor. My dresser drawer was open, and I could see paper money hanging from it. I got out of bed and gathered it up, wondering how it got there and what it meant. I dressed and went downstairs, my fists full of bills. There were people everywhere. I didn't recognize them but soon found out they were mostly men from the *Pendleton*. I knew then it was not a dream that I had experienced.

I took the money to Mr. Cluff. He explained that those on the *Pendleton* that had salvaged some of their belongings before abandoning the stricken vessel had taken a collection to be given as a gift to the Coast Guard crew that had rescued them. This money eventually would go toward the purchase of a television set for the Chatham lifeboat station, a luxury unheard of for a station in those days.

Chief Bangs, with his Chatham crew, and Ralph Ormsby, with his Nantucket crew, arrived at Stage

Harbor during the morning. They were a beat up, worn-out-looking lot of men when they arrived at the station. They had persisted out in the elements of the great northeast storm longer than any of us. We rejoiced at their return.

Transportation arrived, and those SS *Pendleton* survivors who were able to leave were taken to Boston. I would not see or hear from any of them until thirty-two years later.

The ensuing days after the SS *Pendleton*/SS *Fort Mercer* disasters were full of frenzy for the men of Chatham lifeboat station and the town of Chatham. Newspaper reporters and wire services were busy spreading the word about what was now called the Two Tanker Gale. There was considerable discussion about what caused the two great ships to break apart at the same time. Also, the talk went on about who were heroes, who were the near heroes, who had tried, and those who had died. This talk went on for days and months to come.

Thousands of people drove down to the bluff at Chatham to take a look offshore in order to view the remains of the *Pendleton*, still visible in the far distance. Chatham was overwhelmed by this invasion. Up until then, the town was known only to a select few out-siders who had not spread the word about this place, wanting to keep it for themselves.

The Chatham people at first enjoyed the notoriety that the incident brought to town. They were proud of the part the townspeople played in aiding the *Pendleton* survivors. They felt good about themselves, knowing

The bow of the Pendleton, *floating off Chatham on the day after the accident when the tanker broke in half in mountainous seas. (Photo by Richard C. Kelsey, Chatham, Massachusetts. www.capecodphotos.com)*

the citizenry rose to the occasion without regard for payment or any personal gain. It was just a case of people wanting to help people.

For the United States government and particularly the US Coast Guard, the *Pendleton/Fort Mercer* incident proved the value of the men and equipment bought with taxpayer's money for the purpose of providing a service to the public. They were elated over the overall success of the event; it had come at a time when a success was much needed. The Coast Guard had previously come in for some harsh criticism. Events that had taken place at other locations hadn't turned out so well, and there was a public outcry. However, the *Pendleton/Fort Mercer* incident turned this situation around and brought renewed faith in and support for the Coast Guard.

As a result, many coastguardsmen were recognized by the government and received medals and commendations for their individual and collective efforts. The commandant of the United States Coast Guard,

Merlin O'Neill, expressed this sentiment in his speech during the decoration of twenty-one coastguardsmen in Washington, DC, on 14 May 1952.

For the lifeboat men of Chatham, the total experience up to the point of receiving their awards at Washington had been overwhelming for them. These were ordinary men trained in and devoted to the ways of the US Coast Guard who felt that they had only done their duty. The recognition they now received would affect each one in a different way

The skipper of the motor lifeboat CG36383, Chief Donald Bangs, and his crew, consisting of Engineman First Class Emory Haynes, Seaman Richard Ciccone, and Seaman Antonio Ballerini received Coast Guard Commendation Medals. It must be remembered that Bangs and his crew were the first ones ordered out on the stormy day of 18 February 1952. Their orders were to proceed to the aid of the *Fort Mercer*. At the point where it was learned that two ships had broken in half, Bangs, then offshore in CG36383, was diverted to the stern section of the *Pendleton*. While Bangs was headed in that direction, a ship offshore standing by the bow section of the tanker *Pendleton* saw a man onboard hanging on to the bridge. Bangs was recalled and directed to head for the bow section of the *Pendleton*. The CG36500 was then ordered out of Chatham and was to proceed to the stern section of the *Pendleton*.

The skipper of the motor lifeboat CG36500, First Class Boatswain's Mate Bernard C. Webber and his

Three Massachusetts coastguardsmen, recipients of the Treasury Department Gold Lifesaving Medal for their participation in the recent SS Fort Mercer *and SS* Pendleton *rescue operations, are congratulated by Senator Leverett Saltonstall of Dover, Massachusetts. Left to right are: Senator Saltonstall; Andrew J. Fitzgerald, Jr., engineman third class, of Whitinsville, Massachusetts; Richard P. Livesey, seaman, of Wilmington, Massachusetts; and Bernard C. Webber, boatswain's mate first class, of Milton, Massachusetts. (US Coast Guard official photo.)*

crew, consisting of Engineman Third Class Andrew Fitzgerald, Seaman Richard Livesey, and Seaman Irving E. Maske, received the coveted Congressional Gold Lifesaving Medal. These men were labeled "heroes." For them, life would become a mixed blessing. As "living heroes," each would react to and handle his newfound status in very different ways. Each one would know the special responsibility and the pressure of being labeled a "hero." Each one would handle it in his own way.

A lonely Coast Guard "hero" sits alone in a Boston hotel room, dressed up, awaiting his next public relations assignment, 1952. (US Coast Guard official photo.)

Boatswain's Mate First Class Bernard Webber at microphone, expressing his appreciation of the Medal of Valor at a banquet as Commandant O'Neill looks on. (US Coast Guard official photo.)

If, on that fateful day in 1952, Donald Bangs and his crewmen had been allowed to continue to the stern of the *Pendleton*, instead of being diverted back to the bow section, the circumstances would have reversed themselves. There would have been a different set of heroes.

As Chief Bangs often expressed to me after the *Pendleton* disaster, his entire operation became tied up in the attempt to save one man in the bow section. Unfortunately, the man jumped too soon as Bangs arrived and was swallowed up in the towering waves.

Of the Gold Crew, as it became known, Bernard Webber and Richard Livesey remained in the Coast Guard and fulfilled a career. Andrew Fitzgerald and Irving Maske chose to accept discharge from the service when their enlistments expired.

Of all those involved in the *Pendleton/Fort Mercer* disasters, the label of hero placed upon me carried a greater responsibility at a time more difficult to live up to than for any of the others. As the coxswain of motor lifeboat CG36500, which was involved in the rescue of thirty-two men from the *Pendleton*, I was singled out. Within days of the incident, I was ordered to make speeches at such places as Kiwanis Clubs, Rotary Clubs, Propeller Clubs, and the like. I was declared "Hero of the Year" by the American Legion and presented a medal. For a very ordinary young man, it was difficult for me to cope with at the time.

Pressures at the lifeboat station as a result of the incident determined that I ask for a transfer. I was transferred to the Coast Guard rescue vessel CG83388 where my respected friend, Chief Frank Masaschi was the officer in charge. While on duty aboard this vessel, I was often ordered away to perform some sort of Coast Guard public-relations function. While there were those who understood this acclaim, there were others who developed animosity toward me. It came with the territory. I grew to understand. Often in the future, those who were in charge of me would test me by assigning tasks that, to a degree, would be a test to see if I continued to measure up.

In time, things would quiet down. I would return to Chatham time and time again. During each period I would serve at Chatham, it became a most certain date with fate.

The Second Return: The Rescue of Joe Stapleton

I returned to Chatham 13 July 1954 and would serve there again until October of 1955. I had been away for over two years on duty at Woods Hole, Massachusetts, aboard a search and rescue vessel CG83388. My respected friend Chief Frank Masaschi was the officer in charge of the vessel, and Chief Warrant Officer Alvin E. Newcomb was the executive officer of the Woods Hole Coast Guard base.

Both men retired from Coast Guard service shortly before I received orders for this second tour of duty at Chatham lifeboat station. However, they both lived in Chatham, and I would be able to visit them and continue to take advantage of their counsel and encouragement.

Miriam and I, with our son Bernard Jr., now lived in North Eastham on the Cape. With the help of her father, who was a carpenter, and several other old-timers, we built a little house on Oak Road. Miriam's sister Gert and my brother-in-law Art Benner lived next door. Next to them, Art's brother Louie and wife, Dot Benner, would build a place. Other relatives were close by. I was by now truly among the real Cape Codders. As a property owner, with roots dug deep by marriage and service on Cape Cod, a city boy was finally accepted.

At the lifeboat station, there had been many changes during the two years I had been gone. Jim O'Brien was the chief in charge. I previously had served with him at Gay Head. Jim was one of the old breed of surfmen and retired soon after my arrival. He remained in Chatham for his retirement years. Jim was replaced by Chief "Moon" Madison, a local Chatham man who arrived from duty at Point Allerton station at Hull, Massachusetts. Moon was a big man. He had brothers even bigger, thus the names of Full Moon, Quarter Moon, etc., were given to designate which brother one was talking about. Moon became ill while serving at Chatham, retired, and soon thereafter passed away.

Moon's retirement brought Chief Ralph Ormsby from duty at Brant Point lifeboat station on Nantucket to Chatham. He would now take charge of the station. Ralph was on the *Pendleton* rescue also. He took a thirty-six-foot motor lifeboat out of Nantucket the day the *Pendleton* and *Mercer* split in half. Ralph and his crew fought the gale for hours, making slow progress from Nantucket to the Chatham area. Of all those involved in the *Pendleton/Mercer* efforts, Ralph and his crew probably suffered the most. The trip they were required to make was not only the longest but also the most hazardous. Ralph and his crew received commendation medals for their efforts.

I enjoyed this tour at Chatham and liked working under Ralph. He lived in Eastham too, so we had two things in common—our residences and the *Pendleton*.

This tour at Chatham went smoothly. The routine of servicing the lightships, towing in disabled fishing vessels, and answering other types of distress calls was the norm. The CG36500 and other boats based at Chatham were kept very busy. Nothing out of the ordinary happened until one day in March.

The incident took place on one of those cold, clear days, typical of February and March on Cape Cod. The ocean swell ran high offshore but was smooth with wide spaces between the hills of salt water. On Chatham Bar, breakers were evident. The tide running out against the incoming ocean swells caused the two to meet on the shallows of the bar and collide in a foaming mass.

The Chatham fishing fleet had gone out that morning. Most of them returned by midafternoon, cutting their trips short as they were aware of developing conditions at the bar. As the afternoon wore on, all the boats had returned except Joe Stapleton's. The watch in the Chatham lifeboat station tower scanned the offshore waters. A vessel was observed to the northeast of Pollock Rip Lightship and appeared to be heading toward Chatham.

After a time, when the boat was closer, it was determined to be Joe's. The green color of his boat and the way the smoke came out of his engine exhaust left no question. I knew Joe fished alone. He was kind of a quiet guy, friendly enough, but never said too much.

For reasons I could not explain, I found myself asking Chief Ormsby if I could take the motor lifeboat CG36500 out to meet Joe and escort him into Chatham.

Ralph looked at me and pondered my request; after a moment, he gave his approval.

My crew and I left the station. In no hurry, we made our way leisurely down to the fish pier in the station truck. Upon arrival, we rowed out to the lifeboat CG36500, which was resting on its mooring in the harbor. The engine, once started, billowed white smoke in the brisk air. Departing the mooring, we slowly headed out Aunt Lydia's Cove and moved along Old Harbor, passing by Chatham Bars Inn and then the Coast Guard station. The sun was sitting just atop the Chatham Lighthouse, making a grand sight.

As we neared Morris Island and looked toward the east through a break in the dunes of North Beach, the ocean came into view. From this vantage, we could now see Joe Stapleton's boat moving along the outside. We continued along in the CG36500 heading toward the Chatham Bar.

Near the bar, breaking seas became more evident. I stopped the CG36500 and waited. I expected that shortly I would see Joe Stapleton's boat heading on in. At the time, I didn't particularly desire to go out into the breakers. After all, Joe must be all right, we had just seen his boat a few moments ago.

I waited another minute or two, then called the station on the lifeboat's radio to ask lookout tower if they had sight of Joe Stapleton's boat coming in over the bar. The reply came back negative. The tower indicated that the lookout had previously observed Joe heading in over the bar, then lost sight of him in the surf.

Not waiting any longer, I put CG36500's engine in gear and revved her up—heading into the sea on the bar. She began climbing up, over, and through the breakers until we reached the deep outside waters after crossing the bar. The sea then smoothed off into large swells. We looked all around. There was no Joe and no boat! The ocean around us was bare. Where had they gone? What could have happened? It wasn't possible they could have gotten by us.

I called the station again, and they confirmed that no boat was in view from the lookout tower. By now, the sun was setting, and it was getting darker. The CG36500 was in gear, moving slowly by itself, unattended. We strained our eyes looking for signs of Joe and his boat. CG36500's course was her own as my hand was not on the wheel. Suddenly, up ahead off the bow was a dark shadow in the water. I stopped CG36500's engine close to that spot. Peering over the side, I saw what came as a terrible shock.

There, just under the surface, about three feet down, was Joe's boat, bow up, facing us. As the swells rose and fell, so did his boat, remaining just under the surface. I thought to myself, "Good Lord, Joe's boat has sunk, and he is trapped below in it." If that were the case, I knew there was no sense trying to retrieve him as he would be drowned by this time.

I called the station and told Chief Ralph Ormsby about the situation. As it was getting dark, I didn't know if the chief wanted me to grapple Joe's boat and attempt to drag it over the bar to the harbor, or just mark the spot and await tomorrow's daylight.

Meanwhile, once again, CG36500 was moving on its own. I was not steering. It was just in gear going around in slow circles until we made a decision about what we were going to do next.

On her own, CG36500 veered out of the circle and headed in a southerly direction. I didn't pay much attention and didn't bother to change its new course. We were just standing by, awaiting orders. Suddenly one of my crewmen yelled, "Hey, there's something in the water up ahead." I grabbed CG36500's steering wheel and sped up the engine. As I looked ahead I thought I saw what appeared to be a wooden bait tub. As we got closer, we were sure that was what it was, and we knew it must have come from Joe's boat. Another object was spotted in the near darkness. I headed now for that.

As the CG36500 got close, I couldn't believe my eyes. There in the water along side of us was Joe Stapleton. He had a lifejacket clutched to his chest and was rising and falling in the ocean swells. His eyes were wide open and in a wild state; otherwise he was expressionless, a quietness about him. There was no recognition from him that we were even there.

With our boathook, we grabbed ahold of Joe and pulled him over the side of the CG36500. We all leaned out over the rails and dragged his limp form aboard. He said nothing. From all appearances, he was dead. However, we knew he was alive as he released the lifejacket once aboard the lifeboat. We took him immediately below to the forward cabin. Each of us took off outer clothing and wrapped Joe in it. My crew started rubbing him down as I headed CG36500 in over the bar.

When we arrived at the fish pier, an ambulance was waiting to take Joe to the hospital. He suffered from exposure but was released and back down at the Chatham Fish Pier a few days later. When he would see me, he would nod but say nothing. I don't know why; it's just one of those things that happen between seamen when a life-or-death situation has been experienced. It just isn't talked about.

Joe had told the other fishermen that when he was navigating in over Chatham Bar that day, a sea came up behind his boat and broke over the stern, filling the cockpit full of water. In a swamped condition, Joe was able to turn his boat around and start to head back out over the bar. However, the weight of the water in the boat caused it to go down stern first. All he could do was grab a nearby lifejacket and hang on to it, floating clear as the boat sank beneath him.

The amazing part of the story is that the CG36500 on its own, unattended, not only led us to Joe's boat but later to Joe. Perhaps this could be another reason Joe never talked about the matter. I think he felt that it was a matter between himself, the CG36500, and God; that we were only part of the cast.

Not long after the incident with Joe Stapleton, I was promoted to chief boatswain's mate and transferred to Nauset lifeboat station in Eastham, Massachusetts, to serve as the officer in charge of that station. I was happy about the promotion and pleased to be able to serve for a while in my hometown. In the back of my mind, I knew somehow, once again, I would return to Chatham. Further, there would be a reason for it, I was sure.

The Third Return

I returned to Chatham during April 1960. I would begin my third tour of duty at the lifeboat station, this time as a chief boatswain's mate. I would serve as the officer in charge.

When I left in 1955, I knew I would return. The station fascinated me, and somehow it seemed I was destined to be involved in other unusual circumstances.

On my first tour, the *Pendleton* was an unusual event. The second tour was the saving of Joe Stapleton under unusual conditions. My suspicions would prove correct. I would indeed become involved in situations that seem peculiar to this Chatham station.

During the five years I had been gone from Chatham, I served at the Nauset lifeboat station and the Race Point lifeboat station. I was further transferred to a Coast Guard Tug, the CG64301, operating out of Southwest Harbor, Maine. After that, I was assigned to the Nantucket Lightship. My return now to Chatham was a welcome change, and I felt I was home.

The lifeboat station was quite different from when I last served here. There were no familiar faces, more men were assigned to this station than before, and it now was the headquarters for the Coast Guard Group

Commander Cape Cod. Chief Warrant Officer Merritt O. Wright was the group commander and maintained his office within the lifeboat station.

As the officer in charge, I not only had to run the lifeboat station but also had many extra duties to perform for the group commander. I think all the men felt a bit of strain with Mr. Wright on hand all the time.

"M.O.," to those who outranked him or those who were not associated with the Coast Guard, was a special character. When they made him, they threw the mold away. He came from Maine and had served nearly thirty years, mostly on buoy tenders. This may explain some of his peculiarities—of which there were many.

He kept his hair in a crew cut, and with his Bob Hope–type nose, we likened him to "Smilin' Jack," of the comic-strip fame. In fact, he flew a plane and had a pilot's license. M.O. was crude. He always had a big cigar in his mouth. . .and was chewing. . .on the end. He would get someone's attention when his back was toward him by biting off a piece of cigar and spitting it at the person. More often than not, he hit the individual square on the back of the neck.

M.O. also had a peculiar way of handling personnel or administering his commands. As an example, if a new man was sent by the district office for assignment to duty within Group Cape Cod, M.O. had his own special system to determine where he would place the individual.

Usually, the new man was asked if he knew how to shoot pool. M.O. wouldn't even wait for his answer. He would direct the man to the station basement, where the pool table was located. For a small wager, they would play a game of pool. Now, what the individual didn't know was that M.O. played by what he called Machias Rules, taken from the name of a town in Maine. What this meant was that the rules were M.O.'s, designed for the moment.

If the new man persisted in winning, M.O. would indicate the possibility existed that the individual stood a good chance of being assigned to one of the light-ships offshore. If the man lost the game to M.O., he stood a better chance at one of the shore stations on Cape Cod. So it went, and the message would be very clear.

M.O. was well liked in town by the local fishermen. He spent considerable time down at the fish pier, adjusting compasses on their boats, for a fee, of course. He lived in Chatham at this time and went home every night, usually in time to catch the "Guiding Light" on television. This was the only break we got, a bit of relaxation in the evenings.

Chatham station was better now in many ways than it had been in the past. The men only remained on the stations for six days, then received two days off. There was a good television set, a pool table, and other things for the men to do in the little spare time they had. The station was a very busy place still, with a lot of rescue work and an odd assortment of duties directly or indirectly related to the group commander's office located within. For instance, we were required by M.O. to maintain a standard higher than any of the other units. We were the example, so to speak. Our efforts paid off in that for three years running we received an excellent rating from Coast Guard headquarters' inspectors. The personal strain of it all often came out in the men in some odd ways. I must admit I, too, felt the pressure and became involved in a prank or two as evidenced by the following.

Lookout-Tower Lover

During the period I was in charge at Chatham lifeboat station, it was my nightly habit to go up into the lookout tower prior to turning in. I would visit with the man on watch, check out the equipment, and scan the horizon with binoculars to view the flashing of aid-to-navigation lights offshore. I wanted to assure myself all was in order before going down to bed.

One particular night, I was about to start my climb up the lookout tower steps when I heard an unusual amount of scrambling and bustling about coming from the tower house above me. I thought the man on watch above was probably goofing off. Hearing me approach on the steps below, he knocked over the wastebasket. I didn't make any more out of it in my mind, at the time.

Near the top of the tower, the trap door was flung open for me by the man on watch. I climbed up through the hatch and closed it behind me. I sensed the young man was a bit flustered. He said, "Hi Chief, everything all right?" I replied, "Sure, how's it going with you?" However, I knew something was bothering him, and I couldn't put my finger on what it might be.

Lowering the top section of one of the tower

windows, I picked up the binoculars and rested my elbows on the sill. Through the binoculars, I began to scan the offshore area. After watching the various lights for a while, I put the binoculars down and continued to look out the tower window, enjoying the night air. My eyes just happened to glance downward. I was startled to see what appeared to be a human form sprawled out below me, lying on the lookout-tower platform that ran around the outside.

I then knew what had been bothering the man on watch. The longer my eyes focused on the form below, the clearer it became. I noticed it was a female, and then I recognized it as one of the local girls who had been dating the man on watch.

Now I had a problem. The Coast Guard had a very strict policy against women being allowed on one of their stations. The fact that the girl was up in the lookout tower with the man on watch made it even worse. In fact, it would be considered a court-martial offense. I thought about my early days at Chatham, when, in 1948, "Mother Newcomb" was in charge. How he roamed the yard at night with flashlight in hand, trying to catch us with one of the local girls. How he made bed checks on us to assure we were aboard the unit.

Times had changed, but one thing that remained was the loneliness and isolation the men felt when restricted for six days at a time to the station grounds. I understood this—having served under even stricter conditions. It's strange, but I was more liberal in my thinking. I didn't particularly agree with many regulations, perhaps because I had served under more stringent conditions.

The problem I now faced and the question I now asked myself was: How do I handle this situation? I liked the man who was on lookout watch. I also liked the girl and knew her family. I didn't want to embarrass either of them. The girl wasn't aware that I noticed her. The man on watch didn't know I was aware of the situation. The Coast Guard certainly didn't need the publicity that exposing them would bring.

Finally, I figured out what I would do. For a while, I stood talking with the man on watch, just chitchatting. Keeping his attention, I bent down and opened the tower's trap door. I then started down the steps. When I was about ready to close the trap behind me, I paused and said to the seaman. "Say, how about cleaning up the tower, especially around the outside platform, you know, pick up anything not belonging there." I then closed the hatch, not even waiting for his reply.

I then went directly down the tower and into the station building. There, I waited in the shadows, watching out of a window. Sure enough, within minutes, down she came from the lookout tower, ran across the yard, though the gate, and off into the night.

I called the seaman up in the tower from the station phone. I let him know I appreciated him cleaning up the tower this time of night and, further, that I was turning in.

Air Mail, Chatham Style

I, too, often felt the pressures of prolonged duty at Chatham lifeboat station, especially during the period in which it was the Group Command Headquarters. There were times when I would devise pranks or schemes to relieve tension.

One incident stands out. Gene Love worked for the US Postal Service and delivered mail daily to the Chatham lifeboat station. It was his routine to arrive with the mail at the station shortly after we had eaten our lunch. Generally, several of us were gathered in the station office, holding a meeting to plan out the remainder of the day's activities.

Through the office window, we would see Gene walking along past Captain Pennypacker's house and the monument outside the station at the far end of the station yard. He always had the leather mailbag slung over his shoulder and walked with a peculiar stride, perhaps from the weight of his load. Gene would arrive at the station gate and fling it open with a flare, then kick it shut behind him. You could hear the clop of his feet on the wooden walkway leading up to the station's front door. Once inside, Gene would have a few snide remarks about "The Hooligans, Shallow Water Sailors," and other things like that. All in good fun, of course.

I thought about Gene and this everyday occurrence. This was such a routine experience that it was boring for all of us. I decided to spice things up a bit and provide a grand welcome for Gene next time he arrived with the mail.

Ed Ferreira was my assistant at the station. I enlisted his aid in a plan I had devised in my mind. My plan called for the use of a Lyle gun we kept on display in the front hall of the station.

Now, a Lyle gun is a rather large brass cannon. It is used in shooting a projectile, with a line attached to it, out to a ship stranded offshore within yards of a beach. To use this gun you had to place small bags of black powder down the barrel.

A firing cap was provided, into which a 22-caliber blank cartridge was placed. A clip with a lanyard attached was placed under the firing cap, which was spring loaded. Normally, with a projectile placed down the barrel, a yank on the lanyard would fire the blank, ignite the powder, explode, and send the projectile off into the distance.

My plan called for a very different operation. The next day with Ed's assistance, we carried the gun over and set it down just inside the front door. I aimed the barrel up into the air. I then put a small charge of powder down the bore, placed the blank cartridge, slipped the clip under, and ran the lanyard along the floor to my office. We then wadded up balls of newspaper and crammed them down the barrel. All was ready for Gene's arrival.

As usual, we had eaten lunch and were gathered in my office. Ed Ferreira was stationed by the front door. Upon my hand signal, Ed was to push open the door and stand aside so I could do my thing.

Soon, Gene was observed walking along on the sidewalk outside the station fence. He opened the gate and closed it in his normal manner and clomped up the wooden walk. When he was about halfway to the front door, I signaled Ed and yanked on the lanyard. The Lyle gun went off with a roar and skidded back several feet on the front-hall floor from the force. From its barrel spewed a red ball of fire that headed up into the air and then disbursed a shower of black, charred, burning paper that rained downward.

I was watching Gene, our mailman. The expression on his face was priceless as he threw the mailbag up in the air and ran backward, much of the mail scattering on the grass. His state of surprise was evident! We went out the front door, laughing; the scene had made our day. However, Gene didn't think it was funny. Later, I would hear about the incident from Paul Carr, the local postmaster. From then on, Gene would approach the station with caution when delivering the mail. He never tarried and had little to say to us. We didn't hear him mention anything about "Hooligans," or "Shallow Water Sailors" again, though we could read his mind.

New Developments

Over the years, the Chatham area provided a proving ground for Man in his ongoing quest of the sea. For personnel at the Chatham lifeboat station, it not only meant the testing of individual stamina, but the testing of Coast Guard equipment as well. The old thirty-six-foot motor lifeboats had proven themselves time and again, operating in the raging seas of such places as Chatham Bar and Pollock Rip. These little boats were designed to operate in heavy seas. Should the occasion arise where they might be turned over in a sea, they were meant to right themselves.

Times were changing. The old thirty-six footers were limited in their range of operations by their little gasoline engines. The use of gasoline also was a safety factor. As it was proved during the *Pendleton* experience, the engine would quit when the boat was subjected to violent motion that would lay it from side to side in extremely heavy seas.

Also gained from the *Pendleton* experience was the knowledge that, on occasion, it becomes necessary to take onboard many survivors from a shipwreck, some who might be suffering from exposure. The thirty-six footers had very limited space for such survivors, and there were no heated compartments or facilities for aiding victims. Although the CG36500 was able to bring back a load of thirty-six men from the *Pendleton*, that could almost be classed as a miracle. In fact, after the *Pendleton*, a few days later, it was tried to load thirty-six people on the boat, and it just couldn't be done.

Ordered to Coast Guard headquarters during November 1961, I was privileged to assist in the evaluation of a newly designed forty-four-foot motor lifeboat. The evaluation consisted of operating the boat in Chesapeake Bay and up the seacoast to Cape May, New Jersey. In November and December, the boat was tested daily under the most severe weather conditions available at the time.

This new forty-four footer was in sharp contrast to the old thirty-six footers like the CG36500. She was built of steel and powered by two GM diesel engines. She had two heated compartments for survivors, with settees and seat belts to hold them safely in during a rough passage. Unlike CG36500, which only had a compass for navigational equipment, the new lifeboat was equipped with depth-finding equipment and several radios with various ranges and frequencies. The boat had an enclosed pilot station and a seat for the helm with a safety belt attached. It was also designed to roll over and come upright again.

At first I couldn't comprehend the new forty-four footer. I wasn't very impressed by it, except for the helpful equipment it carried. After this month-long test, those of us involved returned the vessel to the Coast Guard at Curtis Bay, Maryland, with a very long list of recommended changes. These were not met with enthusiasm by the designers and headquarters personnel involved in the project. I returned to Chatham in time to celebrate Christmas.

I was ordered back to Coast Guard headquarters during April 1962. The prototype forty-four-foot motor lifeboat CG44300 had been modified extensively and was standing by for further tests. I was to take this vessel on a cruise from Curtis Bay, Maryland, southward as far as Cape Hatteras, then proceed northward on a voyage that would take us to Rockland, Maine, then to Chatham. Operating daily, the vessel stopped at every Coast Guard station along the way. Men from these stations viewed the new vessel and tried it out. The trip lasted six weeks. I was now impressed with this vessel and felt it was more than a suitable replacement for the old thirty-six footers.

We kept the prototype CG44300 at Chatham for a year. The First District Headquarters kept us busy, going out in all kinds of weather and conditions, sometimes very far offshore on very long tows. Nothing seemed to bother this vessel, and it showed no signs of rolling itself over. At the end of a year, we took the boat to Boston, where it was loaded on a freighter and transported to Oregon. There, it would receive further testing.

During tests in Oregon, the boat was rolled over successfully in the large breakers common to the west-coast deep-water bars. We knew then that this vessel would become the standard lifeboat for the Coast Guard and replace the faithful old thirty-six footers.

Shortly thereafter at Chatham, the mass burning of the old thirty-six-foot motor lifeboats began. At the water's edge of the Chatham cut-through, some of these boats were torched, their ashes scavenged for the brass from their fittings. It was a heartbreaking sight. I wondered when it would be CG36500's time.

A Breeches Buoy Rescue

One of the most dangerous situations a ship and its crew could find themselves in is to be stranded without power on what is called a lee shore. During a storm especially, when seas run high and breakers along the beach become powerful, both ship and men face almost impossible odds against their survival. This had been the case for centuries, particularly along the shore of places like Cape Cod.

Should a vessel ground out in the surf line that runs along a beach, it would be lifted up and down and pounded until it broke apart. The crews of such vessels often climbed up into the rigging in hopes that when the mast fell, it would fall toward the beach, where they could get off. Some crewmen would jump over the side in hope of swimming ashore. Rarely would these men make it, as they were soon swallowed up in the breaking surf.

Many times, disabled vessels would become stranded on outer shoals. Sometimes these shoals would be located a few hundred yards from a beach. This condition made it even more difficult for man and his ship to survive.

It seemed most such incidents took place during the winter. Many a man froze to death hanging on to the mast of a stranded vessel. Many a body washed ashore on a desolate stretch of beach, the result of jumping from a stricken vessel. Cape Cod certainly had more than its share of such fatalities.

In most cases where strandings take place, it is impossible to reach the vessel or its crew. Other ships or boats cannot get close enough to render aid. To combat the situation, a system called the breeches buoy was developed in the first half of the nineteenth century. The equipment would be rigged between ships or from the shore out to a stricken vessel.

The lifeboat station or shore version of this equipment was carried in a beach cart that was usually towed to the site of a stranded ship. In the old days, it was pulled by man and beast over the sands. In modern times, four-wheel-drive vehicles do the job with ease.

Arriving at the site of a wreck, the equipment was set up. A Lyle gun or brass cannon was filled with small bags of black power, a firing pin was fitted with a blank cartridge, a steel projectile was placed in the barrel of the cannon with a line attached to it. With a lanyard attached to the firing pin, the gun was now ready for use. A yank on the lanyard caused the spring-loaded firing pin to strike the 22-caliber blank cartridge, igniting the powder, and causing an explosion that shot the projectile from the cannon. The idea was to send the projectile with its line out and over the stranded vessel.

Once aboard the vessel, the line was hauled in, a heavier line attached (called a whip line) was then pulled in and, in accordance with instructions, attached to the end of this line. The stranded sailors would fasten it to the mast. A heavier line called a hawser was then hauled out to the wreck, also with instructions as to where to fasten it on the vessel's mast. The hawser was pulled taut from the shore and fastened by a sand anchor or secured to a vehicle, whichever suited the case.

A breeches buoy was sent out to the wreck. This consisted of a life ring or buoy onto which a pair of canvas pants was fitted. This rig was sent out to the stricken vessel, where a survivor would climb into the ring and place his feet into the pants. When ready he would be hauled ashore. The breeches were hauled back out to the ship and the process repeated as many times as it was necessary.

The rescue of crewmen from fishing vessel *Margaret Rose* was accomplished by the use of breeches buoy equipment on 16 January 1962. The method is little known today. The Coast Guard has all but abandoned the equipment and the training of personnel in its use. The success rate of using helicopters for removing seamen from stranded vessels has been so high that little thought is now given to the use of the old breeches buoy equipment.

Off Race Point, Provincetown, the wind was blowing from the northwest at forty-plus miles per hour. It was cold beyond reason. The seas were a mass of white foam off the Race. At 3:30 a.m., the fishing vessel *Margaret Rose*, with seven men aboard, grounded on an offshore shoal about two hundred yards from the beach. The vessel was awash from the seas breaking over her.

A Coast Guard helicopter arrived at the scene at 4:00 a.m. It was unable to remove the survivors due to the violent motion of the fishing vessel as it rolled back and forth in the sea. Race Point lifeboat station dispatched a motor lifeboat. It arrived on scene but was unable to get close enough to the *Margaret Rose* to aid the crewmen aboard. An amphibious vehicle (DUKW) from Race Point lifeboat station was also dispatched. However, it broke down while making the trip over the dunes to the site and remained disabled and useless.

This was the setting and situation whereupon I would be called to proceed from Chatham to Provincetown to render aid. The phone beside my bed at Chatham station rang a little after 4:00 a.m. I automatically knew something was up and tried to clear my mind before picking up the phone. I answered. The party on the other end said, "This is Search and Rescue Headquarters, Boston, we have a distress off Provincetown. The fishing vessel *Margaret Rose* is grounded on an offshore shoal with seven men aboard. Seas are washing over, and it is in danger of breaking up."

The Boston headquarters went on to explain the situation and summed it all up by saying, "Webber, take your crew and get down to Provincetown as fast as you can. Do whatever has to be done to save those men." I acknowledged by telling them we would depart immediately in the Chatham amphibious vehicle (DUKW). Further, I asked that the only beach apparatus (breeches buoy equipment) remaining on Cape Cod be brought from the Cape Cod Canal lifeboat station to the scene at Provincetown.

Hanging up the phone, I woke two of my fellow Chatham crewmen, Daniel Davidson, engineman first class, and Wayne Chapuis, seaman. We all quickly dressed and departed in the Chatham DUKW. The thirty-five-mile drive to Provincetown in the open vehicle during January was a chilling experience. However, it was nothing compared to what we would face later.

We arrived in our DUKW at the beach in Provincetown just at the break of day. I could see the *Margaret Rose* rolling back and forth, with seas crashing up over her. The seven crewmen were up in the fishing vessel's masts hanging on for their lives. The beach cart with the breeches buoy equipment en route from the Cape Cod Canal station had not arrived as yet. I was concerned for the men on *Margaret Rose*, worried that they would freeze to death or otherwise suffer from exposure to the elements.

With no further thought, I drove our amphibious vehicle into the surf heading toward the stricken vessel. The DUKW lifted up in the first sea it encountered. As it went down the other side the next sea rolled over the top of us. We were swamped. The DUKW filled with water and sank to the bottom right there. We were only about a hundred feet from the beach; however, all that remained showing on the DUKW was its windshield. Fortunately, we were washed ashore to the safety of the beach, soaking wet and very much colder.

Our personal discomforts were forgotten almost

immediately. The arrival of the beach cart and its equipment preoccupied my mind. I knew this equipment was the only hope for the crew of the *Margaret Rose*. I also knew I had never used this equipment in a rescue. In fact, during all my years in the Coast Guard, I had only attended two drills where I had seen the equipment in use.

For me especially, the responsibility was great. It was up to me to organize the few coastguardsmen at the scene and rig this age-old equipment. Time was of the essence, and probably we would only have one chance to do it right. I asked the ten or so coastguardsmen on the scene if any of them had experience in rigging the breeches buoy equipment. Now mind you, these men came from three different Coast Guard stations, Chatham, Race Point, and Cape Cod Canal. To a man, the answer came back "no."

There was a reason for this situation. The Coast Guard had been phasing out the breeches buoy equipment for several months. It had been little used in many years, and it was thought that helicopters would take its place. The only apparatus that remained on Cape Cod was at the Canal station. That station was to maintain a crew proficient in its use, should a need arise. We had the equipment at this scene, but none of the proficient men that should have come with it.

Without further ado, I lined the men up on the beach in a row. I told them to listen and remember what I told them; to ask no questions and just do what I said. Going from man to man I would tell one he was a "weather whip," the man standing next would be a "lee whip," and so forth down the line. I felt a little embarrassed by my forcefulness, and I'm sure they took note that perhaps I was nervous.

Together we moved the heavy brass cannon called a Lyle gun, to a vantage point on the beach. I sighted down the barrel, elevating it to what I thought would be sufficient to send a projectile with line attached up and over the *Margaret Rose*. I loaded two ounces of black powder, contained in little bags, down the Lyle gun barrel. Then I gave it two more for good measure. I tied on the line from the faking box to the steel projectile and placed the projectile down the gun barrel. Inserting a blank cartridge under the firing mechanism, and installing the firing clip attached to the lanyard made all in readiness.

I stood back, the firing lanyard in my hand. The rest of the men stood silently by. A brief prayer was offered by me: "God, make this shot good, Amen." I gave the lanyard a pull. It was followed by a great explosion. The Lyle gun jumped up in the air and fell backward in the sand. I saw and heard the whistle of the projectile with its line attached as it headed up and out toward the *Margaret Rose*. The projectile went out of sight toward Boston. However, the line now lay over and aboard the fishing vessel.

The crew on the *Margaret Rose* came to life. Their spirits were raised by the fact that there was now a link between them and the safety of the shore. They hauled in on the small line and we sent out the whip line. It had instructions attached to tell them where to fasten it on their mast. Once the whip line was set on board *Margaret Rose*, we then pulled out the hawser and finished rigging the equipment.

We sent out the ring with breeches attached. It arrived on board *Margaret Rose* and the first man climbed in and was hauled to safety to shore. The coastguardsmen on the lee whip hauled one way, the men on the weather whip hauled the other, back and forth, each time bringing in another survivor from the stricken vessel.

We hauled the breeches offshore six times successfully. Each time we hauled them back, a man would be onboard, sitting in the canvas pants. I was feeling pretty good about the situation as we hauled the buoy off to the *Margaret Rose* in order to retrieve the last man. Suddenly the wind picked up, the seas were higher, and the *Margaret Rose* was violently tossing about. The lines between the ship and shore were first tight then would slack off. We had a difficult time maintaining a balance of tension. We watched as the breeches arrived out at the *Margaret Rose*. We saw the man climb in. Then we heard a crack and saw the mast break off. The mast landed in the water, taking the man and lines attached with it and sweeping them along the beach.

Daniel Davidson and Wayne Chapuis, alert to what had happened, ran down the beach and out into the icy water after the man who was tangled up in the rigging. They reached him, cut him loose, and dragged him to the beach. As a result, all seven men from the *Margaret Rose* were saved. Suffering from exposure, they were taken to Race Point station.

We remained on the beach, picking up our equipment while a Coast Guard helicopter still hovered overhead. The Race Point lifeboat headed back to Provincetown. I thought about it and realized that the old breeches buoy method of rescuing seamen from a stranded vessel was the only one that could have worked in this case.

As for the *Margaret Rose,* shortly after we took the last man off, the batteries on board exploded and she caught fire. However, the flames were put out by seas washing over her. Sometime later, the vessel was pulled off the shoal and taken to Flyer's Boatyard in Provincetown, where it was rebuilt. In the end, *Margaret Rose* lived to fish again.

There is some irony to this story. A few months before the *Margaret Rose* incident, the Coast Guard sent out a questionnaire to all the officers in charge of Coast Guard stations, asking their views about retaining the breeches buoy equipment. At the time, my reply was that I thought it should be retained because it was not only was a good backup method when a helicopter rescue might not work but it was also a good training device that brought men together as a team.

My attitude was criticized. I was referred to as a has-been by some officials. I wasn't modern in my thinking, not progressive in adapting to newer methods, and so forth. Then *Margaret Rose* happened. It was as if I planned it to prove a point. I recommended Davidson and Chapuis for a Silver Lifesaving Medal; it was disapproved. They did receive a letter of appreciation from the Coast Guard district commander.

Chatham lifeboat station, 1960.

Ending the Chatham Adventure

After the *Margaret Rose* incident, I remained in charge at Chatham lifeboat station for one more year. The year was an awkward one for me. It seemed my relations with the group commander deteriorated to the point where he considered I was no longer an asset to him or the station. As a result, I was transferred to the Cross Rip Lightship on August 29, 1963.

In retrospect, I think M.O. Wright, the group commander, was correct in his assessment. However, I knew I had served the Chatham community for eight years of my life starting when I was a very young man. I returned again and again, each time it seemed for a special purpose. From the lowly status of a Coast Guard seamen, I developed to the point where I would eventually serve in charge of the historic Chatham lifeboat station, win the coveted Gold Lifesaving Medal, and above all, realize that I had "done my duty." To some, this may not seem like much of an achievement, but for me, the son of a Baptist minister who left home at the age of sixteen to serve in the Pacific Coast Guard service, particularly the years at Chatham, put meaning into my life that has lasted.

Life after Chatham

I left Chatham lifeboat station for the final time on 29 August 1963. Transferred to the Cross Rip Lightship, I would only serve on that vessel until October, when it was decommissioned.

I was reassigned to the Coat Guard cutter *Point Banks*, which operated also out of Woods Hole. After several months of search and rescue duties aboard this vessel, both ship and crew were ordered to duty in Vietnam.

Returning from service in Vietnam, I was assigned to the Coast Guard buoy tender *Hornbeam*, once again operating out of Woods Hole. Upon my return, taking up new duties, I became aware of new developments that had taken place in the Coast Guard while I was away. The times were turbulent. The Coast Guard had taken a new direction. The politics of the day divided traditional service philosophy.

The values inbred in me over a twenty-one year period no longer seemed to apply or have any relation to the new image that the service was in the process of developing.

As a result, I took retirement from the US Coast Guard 1 September 1966.

Warrant Officer Webber, DaNang, Vietnam, 1965. (Saving lives no longer a prime importance.) (Photo from the Author's collection.)

A New Beginning

After leaving the Coast Guard, I soon found out old Coast Guard "heroes" were not highly sought after by the civilian labor market. Only thirty-eight at the time, my first job was staining newly built beach cottages for Bob Erickson, a local Eastham builder. Using a gray stain, I painted the inside of those cottages most of the winter. There was no heat inside the cottages, and the view from the windows was a frozen Cape Cod Bay. It was very depressing for me, and I missed the sea.

The position of harbormaster for the Town of Wellfleet became available. I applied for the position even though I lived in Eastham. The job became mine, partly I think because my wife Miriam was born and brought up in Wellfleet. I was happy to at least have a connection again with the waterfront.

The meager Coast Guard pension I received and the pay for harbormaster and painting cottages still wasn't enough for four of us to get by on. I knew I had to do something to bring in more money. Phil Deschamps, of the then–Nauset Auto & Marine in Orleans, hired me. I worked for him reconditioning boats. Then I decided to get a boat of my own and run charter trips during the summers out of Rock Harbor, Orleans.

I bought a little wooden thirty-four-foot Maine-built boat named *Sinbad*. A lovable Cape Cod character named Phil Schwind, who had a site at Rock Harbor for many years, was retiring. He helped me obtain his coveted berth at Rock Harbor by putting in a good word for me at the town office in Orleans. I rented his berth from the town and was soon in business. Together, we worked the boat as a family business. My wife booked the trips, my son served as mate onboard, and my little daughter would help clean the boat after the trips. I continued to work for Nauset Marine during the winters. For the next two years, we were very happy. Then, the bottom fell out of the barrel. The boat began to cost more than I made with it. Problems developed, and I knew I had to make more changes.

The opportunity of working for the National Audubon Society at their facility in Maine presented itself. I took the job of Warden and Head Boatman at the Todd Wildlife Refuge and Audubon educational camp in Maine. For four years as a family, we had a wonderful existence working for the society. It presented a great opportunity for us to learn about the environment and to deal with a fine organization.

An upheaval in our lives determined that we make another change. I then went to work for the Hurricane Island Outward Bound School in Maine. I remained for two years as their waterfront department manager. During this period, I would hear of old motor lifeboat CG36500 once again. I had long thought she had been burned along with her sister vessels many years before. Then I received an article in the mail written by Charles Koehler for the *Cape Cod Standard-Times* newspaper on 16 January 1973. The article, entitled "CG36500: Something Special," came as a shock to me. From it, I learned the little lifeboat still existed, but just barely.

CG36500, for some reason, was turned over to the Cape Cod National Seashore park as a gift from the Coast Guard in 1969. It had been brought from Chatham to the Cape Cod National Seashore headquarters in South Wellfleet, where it was set out in a barren field while officials pondered what to do with it. For me, it was as if a long-lost friend had returned into my life. However, I felt helpless, not able to do anything about the situation. From then on, almost daily, I continued to think about that boat and wondered what would happen to her.

Leaving the Outward Bound School, I continued to work in the marine field for dredging companies, towboat companies, salvage companies—I even served a stint with the Army Corp of Engineers as a marine construction inspector. Eventually, I wound up in Florida, where for the past seven years I was employed by the Belcher Towing Company of Miami. After forty-two years of work on the sea, it became time to come home. I left Belcher in order to complete this work before moving on to new horizons.

The Clock

The rebirth of old Coast Guard motor lifeboat CG36500 at Rock Harbor, Massachusetts, in June of 1982 meant that the legend would continue. As she travels forth on the waters of her native environment, she spreads the message of past human endeavors. She also represents the current achievement of people who have an appreciation for their heritage and feel the need to retain traditional values. The construction of the little vessel is a prime example of the skills and craftsmanship performed by men dedicated to the perfection of their trade. Also, her exploits over the many years of service under the control of very ordinary men maintained the standard for which the US Coast Guard became famous.

Paying my respects to the gallant vessel, on this particular day of her rebirth, I had come prepared for one more task. I felt this was appropriate before Miriam and I departed on our long journey home.

Telephoning Charles H. Thomsen, the President of the Orleans Historical Society at his home in Orleans, I told him that there was something that I wanted to do before I left Cape Cod. Without further explanation, I asked that he meet me at the home of my sister-in-law and her husband, Gertrude and Arthur Benner, located on Oak Road, North Eastham. Charlie agreed to the meeting and stated he would be down around seven o'clock.

In the meantime, I had gathered at my in-laws' home, relatives who were native Cape Codders. I felt that they should share the experience of what I was about to do. After all, they had a vested interest in CG36500 and what this book is all about. So, too, does the reader.

Charlie Thomsen arrived at North Eastham as promised. I met him outside when he arrived and invited him in. I introduced him to those present and ushered him into a chair located in the corner of the living room. I then explained to Charlie and the others that I had previously made a tape recording that I wanted them all to hear. Further, that I had brought a gift with me that I wished to present to the Orleans Historical Society. The gift wasn't wrapped. I had placed it in a simple brown paper bag. Handing the bag to Charlie, I requested he hold it in his lap until an appropriate moment during the playing of the tape. Formality out of the way, I pushed the play button on the tape player. This was the message I wanted to express.

• • •

Occasion of Presenting Clock from Pendleton
Given in tape form to Orleans Historical Society

President Thomsen, Friends of Orleans Historical Society,

Your society and its work is one of which you can be justly proud. The recent undertaking of the "Rescue 36500" project is an example of the real American guts it takes to overcome government, state, and financial obstacles, through community spirit, in order to retain a part of our heritage.

As a young man, in 1946, I came to Cape Cod to serve in the US Coast Guard. My association with older coastguardsmen, local fishermen, and Cape Cod people in general instilled in me an appreciation for human values and for what was real. I learned to respect the elements and further developed a sense for God. The proud heritage Cape Codders displayed made an impression of me and made me want to be part of and live up to the traditions of the Cape and its people.

Some six years later, I was put to the test. In early 1952, I was called upon to do what traditionally had been done by many Cape Codders before me. It was a proud heritage I had to live up to. I am happy to say, inspired by this heritage and with help from God, I was able to live up to the true traditions of Cape Cod sea-faring men. Names, or individual deeds, are not what is important. Yours is the greater deed in keeping alive the heritage that is so necessary for the human connection. May the CG36500 in its continued voyage carry with it a message of inspiration, hope, and the tradition which is all ours and so necessary for human existence.

I salute you all for your works and ask that God bless all your endeavors.

Now, if you would bear with me, I have but one more thing to do.

I have brought with me something that I would like to present to the society. Before doing so, stay with me while I tell you a story which relates to this presentation.

Within a few days of the wreck of the Pendleton in 1952, as soon as the seas subsided, some of the local seafaring folk, known affectionately to me as The Chatham Pirates, clambered aboard the remains of the broken stern section.

Rumor had it of items found aboard, and the stories ran high about the finds. Although closed-mouthed secrecy prevailed as the order of the day, for fear there might be some government or salvage claim, certain items stood out as cherished souvenirs and were talked about in hushed voices.

At the time, I had heard the rumors, and I must admit I was envious because I had no souvenir— no remembrance from the Pendleton. As I was a member of the Coast Guard at the time, I never dared to go near the remains for fear of being caught and court-martialed should I take the least little thing.

Some fourteen years later, shortly before retiring from the Coast Guard, I had an experience which meant a great deal to me. It had a great effect on my life, and I would like to share it with you now. Coming home from Coast Guard service in Vietnam in the early part of 1966,

I found myself disillusioned, depressed, confused, out of touch with people, politics, and the Coast Guard—which I had served for nearly twenty-one years.

I was assigned to the Coast Guard cutter Hornbeam *at Woods Hole and existed in that mental state until one night in April.*

Friends from Eastham suggested that my wife and I accompany them on an outing to Hyannis. I was reluctant to go, but in the end conceded.

Later, upon returning to Eastham, our friends suggested stopping in a local Eastham restaurant. Upon arriving at the restaurant and seeing the large amount of cars parked outside, I suggested that we go to our house rather than stop. Our friends in whose car we were riding said, "No, we're going to stop in."

Upon entering the restaurant, I was amazed at the crowd of people that were there and that there were so many familiar faces. I said to my wife, "What do you think is going on here?" She pointed up to a sign that I had not noticed. It said "Welcome Home, Bernie." Then I knew. Yes, it was a welcome home party. Needless to say, I was overwhelmed. The party progressed with the usual camaraderie and human emotions of such an event.

Out of the crowd, a man walked up to me. He was an older man dressed in a wool overcoat and felt hat. He was clutching a brown paper bag under his arm.

I then recognized him when he spoke as Harold Claflin, former harbormaster of Chatham. He said, "Welcome home, Bernie," while thrusting the brown paper bag he was carrying into my arms, saying further, "Here, this rightfully should be yours. I've had it for many years, since just after the shipwreck of the Pendleton."

As I reached into the bag, I knew what Harold had given to me. I recognized it immediately as the ship's clock off the broken stern section of the Pendleton. He had obtained it just a few days after the disaster.

When I looked up, Harold was gone. He had left as quickly as he had arrived. I never saw him again, but I cherish the relationship I had in working with and learning from Harold Claflin while he was harbormaster at Chatham. At the moment, I felt no man had received a greater gift or tribute than I. Not only was I welcomed home by friends and neighbors, but I received such a cherished possession from a dear friend and comrade.

President Thomsen, members of the Orleans Historical Society, I would like now to present to you this clock which lived its days on board the Pendleton and witnessed the life and death of that vessel. It rightfully belongs on Cape Cod and in the possession of Cape Codders who traditionally rise to the occasion of humans in need.

When the tape ended, Charlie reached into the old brown paper bag and took out the clock from the tanker SS *Pendleton*. There was a glimmer of moisture in his eyes. It had survived the ravages of time and still ticked away, refusing to give in. So, too, does that old lifeboat named only CG36500. The lifeboat men and people of Chatham may be different now, living more-sophisticated lives. However, for them, as it was for those of us in bygone days, remains a heritage to build on. One thing for certain, the surrounding waters will continue to be an influence in their lives.

Chatham Revisited

The occasion of my daughter Patricia's wedding brought Miriam and me back to Cape Cod. Patricia desired to procure her marriage license in the town where she was born and to be married on Cape Cod. As parents, we were proud to honor her request.

On the twenty-ninth of April, Patricia was married at the Captain Linnell House in Orleans. The freighter *Eldia* was ashore at Nauset Beach, which seemed most fitting for the occasion. Among the sixty or so guests gathered for the ceremony were represented a cross-section of Cape Cod and New England people, including seafarers the likes of fishermen and tugboat captains, bankers, builders, school teachers, and even a noted marine historian and photographer. As I looked around the room at the people who had gathered there, I felt nostalgic.

Patricia (Webber) Hamilton after her wedding at the Capt. Linnell House, Orleans, Mass. She is holding up a T-shirt with a picture of the freighter ELDIA ashore at Orleans. (Photo by William P. Quinn.)

A day or so after the wedding, I drove to Chatham alone and parked across the street from the Coast Guard station. The following thought came to me.

Standing at this Chatham Bluff alone
Returning to this place I once called home
While staring out upon the sea
It brought back memories of them again for me.
I thought about the Landry's *crew and of*
   Archie-Elroy-Tiny and the others gone
   on Pendleton, *too.*
Souls lost the price to pay, of wrecked and sunken
   vessels in which men had no say.

We coastguardsmen tried again and again,
   and with success from the tanker Pendleton.
Brought back thirty-two men.
Then there was Joe Stapleton, you see.
He made thirty-three.

Oh, there were more I'm sure, but there's no
   way to even the score.
Chatham remains a place where people still try,
Coast Guards and town folk ready to help
So that seamen won't die.
The old motor lifeboat 36500 by name
Is still here to remind us
The sea plays a deadly life-and-death game.
Serving this town meant so much to me.
My memories are dear.
I'll return again someday to gaze out upon the sea.

Charles W. Bridges

Thirty–two years after the *Pendleton* incident, I received a telephone call at my home in Cocoa, Florida. The call came from a fellow by the name of Charles W. Bridges. He went on to tell me that he was one of the survivors from the tanker SS *Pendleton*. Further, he said that he was only eighteen at the time and the youngest of those saved. Charlie went on to tell me that shortly after his rescue, he joined the Coast Guard and made the service a career.

Later, I was to meet Charlie face to face. He works aboard a research vessel now for the University of Miami. At the time, I worked aboard a tug at Port Canaveral, Florida. One morning, I saw Charlie Bridges's ship enter Port Canaveral Harbor and tie up to a pier. I walked up the dock to see if Charlie was on board. As I headed toward the ship, an individual was heading toward me. When we were close to each other, I looked at the man and he looked at me. There was a sort of magnetism that took place. I knew it was Charlie Bridges, and he knew it was me, although there was nothing visual that we could recognize about each other.

Charlie asked me aboard the research vessel for a cup of coffee. We sat down and talked for awhile. The captain of Charlie's ship passed by where we were sitting. Charlie stopped him and introduced me to him, saying, "Captain, this is the man I told you about before. He's the one who piloted the Coast Guard motor lifeboat CG36500 back in 1952 and saved my life."

The words Charlie expressed at that time meant more to me than anything that has transpired in my life during the past thirty-two years.

APPENDIX A: THE RESTORATION

THE CG36500 WAS ACQUIRED IN 1981 by the Orleans Historical Society, and in November, the boat was moved to Orleans. The restoration by volunteers was completed in six months. Over $10,000 was donated to the restoration fund by interested persons far and wide. On June 22, 1982, the boat was launched at Rock Harbor in Orleans and is now a floating museum, plying the waters of southern New England on summer cruises to selected ports in Massachusetts and Rhode Island.

Fred Crowell of Harwich donated the use of his crane to lift the boat out of the scrub pines and lowered onto a trailer for the trip to Orleans. (Photo by William P. Quinn.)

The entire hull had to be scraped down to bare wood. Fiske Rollins wielded a scraper to help bring the hull back to pristine condition. (Photo by William P. Quinn.)

In May, the boat was again placed on the trailer and brought out of the warehouse, ready to float. The CG36500 was launched at Rock Harbor in Orleans in June 1982.

Bernie Webber, June 22, 1982 at Rock Harbor, Orleans, MA on the 36500. This was just before it was launched after restoration.

There were several hundred spectators at the ceremony who broke into applause when Webber climbed aboard. Webber said, "What makes me happy is to see the community spirit."

The CG36500 at Rock Harbor, Orleans, photographed by Marcia Bromley, 2015.

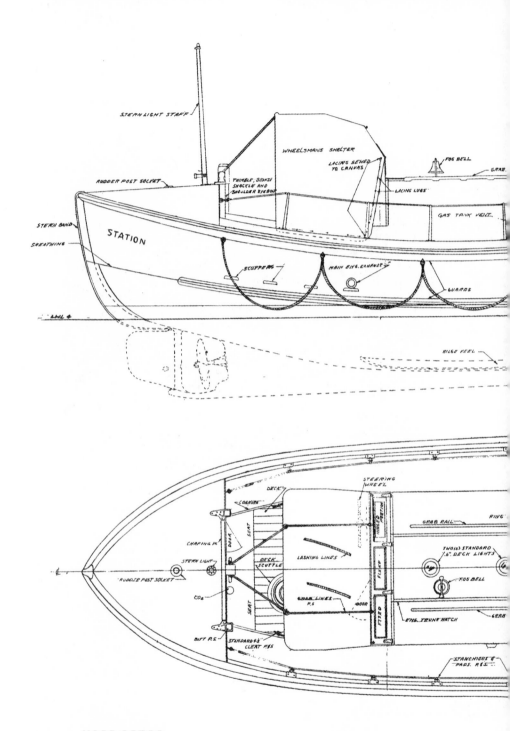

USCG 36500

The 36-foot motor lifeboat is equipped with a 2,000 pound bronze keel to enable the boat to roll over and recover upright.

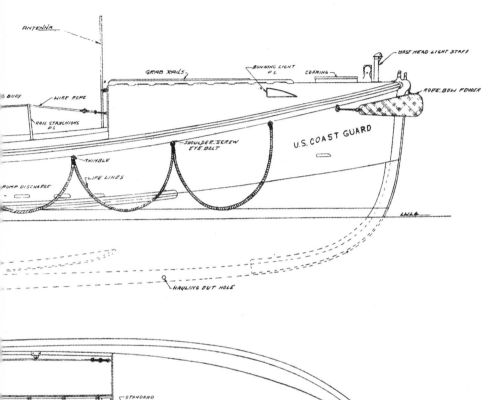

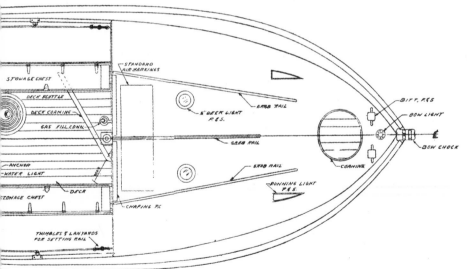

SPECIFICATIONS

Length overall	36 ft., 8 in.	Weight	20,000 lbs.
Beam	10 ft., 8 in.	Speed	8 knots
Draft	3 ft., 5 in.	Range	200 miles

★ ★ ★

COVER ART FOR *Into A Raging Sea* comes from Tony Falcone's painting *Rescue of the Pendleton* by the 36500, which also appears on page 90. The painting is one of a series of works that comprise the US Coast Guard's *Historical Murals Project*, located in Waesche Hall at the USCG Academy in New London, CT. Falcone has written, "As a painter, I can not imagine a more satisfying artistic process than to have the subject of your artwork work along side of you, recalling an event of over sixty years ago, sharing his memory of that onsite experience: that exact night—the storm, the darkness, the crashing waves, and mostly the determination that he and his crew would indeed bring those stranded back to safety. As we worked together on the development of this theme, both at the studio and through mailed sketches and phone calls, I came to understand that just as Bernie brought the scene alive for me, I was in a strange way, once again making it alive for him, on canvas. As the painting neared completion and he and his wife, Miriam, were leaving my barn studio early one evening after giving final approval, Bernie turned one last time, just as I had turned out the lights—leaving the painting illuminated only by the faintest evening light—and exclaimed, "That's it!"

For more information on Tony Falcone's artwork, please visit: www.falconeartstudio.com.